Evidence-Based Instruction in Reading

A Professional Development Guide to Culturally Responsive Instruction

Robin Wisniewski

Baldwin-Wallace College

Gay Fawcett

Kent State University

Nancy D. Padak

Kent State University

Timothy V. Rasinski

Kent State University

Boston   Columbus   Indianapolis   New York   San Francisco   Upper Saddle River
Amsterdam   Cape Town   Dubai   London   Madrid   Milan   Munich   Paris   Montreal   Toronto
Delhi   Mexico City   São Paulo   Sydney   Hong Kong   Seoul   Singapore   Taipei   Tokyo

Vice President, Editor-in-Chief: Aurora Martínez Ramos
Editorial Assistant: Meagan French
Photo Research: Annie Pickert
Managing Editor: Central Publishing
Project Manager: Laura Messerly
Art Director: Jayne Conte
Cover Designer: Karen Salzbach
Cover Image: Getty Images
Production Management: Saraswathi Muralidhar/PreMediaGlobal
Composition: PreMediaGlobal
Text Printer/Bindery: Courier/Stoughton
Cover Printer: Courier/Stoughton
Text Font: 11/13 Giovanni Book

Credits and acknowledgments for materials borrowed from other sources and reproduced, with permission, in this textbook appear on the appropriate page within the text.

Library of Congress Cataloging-in-Publication Data

Evidence-based instruction in reading: a professional development guide to culturally responsive instruction/Robin Wisniewski . . . [et al.].
    p. cm.
  Includes bibliographical references.
  ISBN-13: 978-0-13-702215-1
  ISBN-10: 0-13-702215-8
 1. Language arts—Social aspects—United States.   2. Literacy—Social aspects—United States.
3. Multicultural education—United States. I. Wisniewski, Robin. II. Title.
  LB1576.E93 2012
  370.1170973—dc22

                                                 2010052041

10 9 8 7 6 5 4 3 2 1

www.pearsonhighered.com

ISBN-10:   0-13-702215-8
ISBN-13: 978-0-13-702215-1

Among us, we have been teachers and teacher educators for more than 100 years! During this time, we have developed deep and abiding respect for teachers and trust in their ability to offer their students the very best possible instruction. Yet we also agree with librarian John Cotton Dana (1856–1929), who said, "Who dares to teach must never cease to learn."

Our careers have been marked by continual learning. We dedicate this book to all who have taught us and all whom we have taught—all who have dared to teach.

RW
GF
NP
TR

About the Authors

Robin Wisniewski is an Assistant Professor of Education at Baldwin-Wallace College, where she directs the Leadership in Higher Education graduate program. As a licensed psychologist and nationally certified school psychologist, her major interests, specialties, and teaching areas are the psychology of learning and leadership. She frequently works with teachers and school leaders and has taught and led over 100 courses and workshops in various areas such as standardized and authentic assessment, program evaluation and research, diversity and cultural responsiveness, identity development, counseling, K–12 and college literacy, educational intervention, and curriculum development. A graduate of Kent State University, Dr. Wisniewski earned bachelor's degrees in business and psychology, graduate degrees in school psychology, a Ph.D. in curriculum and instruction with a focus in literacy, and an equivalency doctorate in school psychology awarded by the Ohio State Board of Psychology.

Gay Fawcett has been in education for over 36 years as a teacher, principal, language arts consultant, and curriculum director. She also directed Kent State University's Research Center for Educational Technology. She currently teaches online and face-to-face courses for four major universities and provides curriculum consultation for schools and school districts. She has authored or co-authored more than 90 articles, books, and book chapters for educational publications including the *Kappan*, *Educational Leadership*, *Language Arts*, *The Reading Teacher*, and others. She served with Drs. Rasinski and Padak as an associate editor of *The Reading Teacher*. Dr. Fawcett earned a bachelor's degree in elementary education and a master's degree in reading from the University of Akron. She was awarded a Ph.D. in curriculum and instruction with an emphasis in literacy from Kent State University. Her dissertation on middle school literacy received three awards, including the Association for Supervision and Curriculum Development's Outstanding Dissertation Award.

Nancy D. Padak recently retired from Kent State University, where she was a Distinguished Professor in the College and Graduate School of Education, Health, and Human Services; Director of Kent State's Reading and Writing Center; and a teacher in the area of literacy education. She is the Principal Investigator for the Ohio Literacy Resource Center, which has provided support for adult and family literacy programs since 1993. Prior to her arrival at Kent State in 1985, she was a classroom teacher and district administrator. She is an active researcher, author, and consultant. She has also served in a variety of leadership roles in professional organizations, including the presidency of the College Reading Association and (with others) the editorship of *The Reading Teacher* and the *Journal of Literacy Research.* Dr. Padak's academic degrees in the Teaching of English and Reading were awarded by the University of Illinois and Northern Illinois University.

Timothy V. Rasinski is a Professor of Education in the Department of Teaching, Leadership, and Curriculum Studies at Kent State University. He teaches graduate and undergraduate courses in literacy education. His major interests include working with children who find reading difficult, phonics and reading fluency instruction, and teacher development in literacy education. He has published over 100 articles and 10 books on various aspects of reading education. Dr. Rasinski is past editor of *The Reading Teacher* and the *Journal of Literacy Research.* He has served as president of the College Reading Association and as a member of the Board of Directors of the International Reading Association. In 2010, Dr. Rasinski was elected to the Reading Hall of Fame. He earned bachelor's degrees in economics and education at the University of Akron and the University of Nebraska at Omaha. His master's degree in special education also comes from the University of Nebraska at Omaha. Dr. Rasinski was awarded the Ph.D. from The Ohio State University.

Contents

CHAPTER 3

*Instructional Strategies for Culturally
Responsive Teaching   45*

CHAPTER 4

Beyond Strategies   83

CHAPTER 5

Resources   107

Series Introduction

Evidence-Based Instruction in Reading: A Professional Development Guide

Better than a thousand days of diligent study is one day spent with a great teacher.

JAPANESE PROVERB

*L*earning to read is perhaps a young child's greatest school accomplishment. Of course, reading is the foundation for success in all other school subjects. Reading is critical to a person's own intellectual development, later economic success, and the pleasure that is found in life.

Similarly, teaching a child to read is one of the greatest accomplishments a teacher can ever hope for. And yet reading and teaching reading are incredibly complex activities. The reading process involves elements of a person's psychological, physical, linguistic, cognitive, emotional, and social world. Teaching reading, of course, involves all these and more. Teachers must orchestrate the individuality of each child they encounter, the physical layout of the classroom and attendant materials, their own colleagues, parents, the school administration, the school's specified curriculum, and their own style of teaching! The popular cliché that "teaching reading is not rocket science" perhaps underestimates the enormity of the task of teaching children to read!

The complexity of teaching reading can be, quite simply, overwhelming. How does a teacher teach the various skills in reading to the point of mastery, while simultaneously attending to the school and state curricular guidelines, using an appropriate variety of materials, and meeting the individual needs of all children in the classroom? Because of this complexity, many schools and districts

xii

SERIES
INTRODUCTION

*Evidence-Based
Instruction
in Reading*

select reading programs to provide the structure and sequence for a given grade level. Following basal reading programs, for example, assures coverage of at least some key skills and content for reading. Yet no single program can be sensitive to the culture of the classroom, school, and community; the individual children in the classroom; and the instructional style of the teacher. Addressing these issues is the teacher's responsibility.

Despite everyone's best intentions, many children have failed to learn to read up to expectations. The results of periodic assessments of American students' reading achievement, most notably the National Assessment of Educational Progress, have demonstrated little, if any, growth in student reading achievement over the past 30 years. And this lack of growth in literacy achievement is at least partially responsible for equally dismal results in student growth in other subject areas that depend highly on a student's ability to read.

The National Reading Panel Report

Having noticed this disturbing trend, the National Reading Panel (NRP) was formed by the U.S. Congress in 1996 and given the mandate of reviewing the scientific research related to reading and determining those areas that science has shown have the greatest promise for improving reading achievement in the elementary grades. In 2000, the NRP came out with its findings. Essentially, the NRP found that the existing scientific research points to five particular areas of reading that have the greatest promise for increasing reading achievement. These are phonemic awareness, phonics and word decoding, reading fluency, vocabulary, and reading comprehension. Additionally, the NRP indicated that investments in teachers, through professional development activities, hold promise for improving student reading achievement.

The findings of the NRP have been the source of considerable controversy, yet they have been used by the federal and state governments, as well as by local school systems, to define and mandate reading instruction. In particular, the federal Reading First program has mandated that any school receiving funds from Reading First must embed within its reading curriculum direct and systematic teaching of phonemic awareness, phonics, reading fluency, vocabulary, and comprehension. The intent of the mandate, of course, is to provide students with instruction that is based on the best evidence that it will have a positive impact on students' reading achievement.

Although we may argue about certain aspects of the findings of the NRP—in particular, what it left out of its report on effective instructional principles—we find ourselves in solid agreement with the panel that the five elements that it identified are indeed critical to success in learning to read.

Phonemic awareness is crucial to early reading development. Students must develop an ability to think about the sounds of language and to manipulate those sounds in various ways—to blend sounds, to segment words into sounds, and so on. An inability to deal with language sounds in this way will set the stage for difficulty in phonics and word decoding. To sound out a word, which is essentially what phonics requires of students, readers must have adequate phonemic awareness. Yet some estimates indicate that as many as 20% of young children in the United States do not have sufficient phonemic awareness to profit fully from phonics instruction.

Phonics, or the ability to decode written words in text, is clearly essential for reading. Students who are unable to accurately decode at least 90% of the words they encounter while reading will have difficulty gaining appropriate meaning from what they read. We prefer to expand the notion of phonics to word decoding. Phonics, or using the sound–symbol relationship between letters and words, is, without doubt, an important way to decipher unknown words. However, there are other methods for decoding written words. These include attending to the prefixes, suffixes, and base elements of longer words; examining words for rimes (word families) and other letter patterns; using meaningful context to determine unknown words; dividing longer words into smaller parts through syllabication; and making words part of one's sight vocabulary, the words that are recognized instantly and by sight. Good readers are able to employ all of these strategies and more. Appropriately, instruction needs to be aimed at helping students develop proficiency in learning to decode words using multiple strategies.

Reading fluency refers to the ability to read words quickly, as well as accurately, and with appropriate phrasing and expression. Fluent readers are able to decode words so effortlessly that they can direct their cognitive resources away from the low-level decoding task and toward the more important meaning-making or comprehension part of reading. For a long time, fluency was a relatively neglected area of the reading curriculum. In recent years, however, we have come to realize that, although fluency deals with the ability to efficiently and effortlessly decode words, it is critical to good reading comprehension and needs to be part of any effective reading curriculum.

xiii

SERIES
INTRODUCTION
*Evidence-Based
Instruction
in Reading*

xiv

SERIES
INTRODUCTION

*Evidence-Based
Instruction
in Reading*

Word and concept meaning is the realm of vocabulary. Not only must readers be able to decode or sound out words, but also they must know what these words mean. Instruction aimed at expanding students' repertoire of word meanings and deepening their understanding of already known words is essential to reading success. Thus, vocabulary instruction is an integral part of an effective instructional program in reading.

Accurate and fluent decoding of words, coupled with knowledge of word meanings, may seem to ensure comprehension. However, there is more to it than that. Good readers also actively engage in constructing meaning, beyond individual words, from what they read. That is, they engage in meaning-constructing strategies while they read. These include ensuring that they employ their background knowledge for the topics they encounter in reading. It also means that they ask questions, make predictions, and create mental images while they read. Additionally, readers monitor their reading comprehension and know when to stop and check things out when things begin to go awry—when readers become aware that they are not making adequate sense out of what they are reading. These are just some of the comprehension strategies and processes good readers use while they read to ensure that they understand written texts. These same strategies must be introduced and taught to students in an effective reading instruction program.

Phonemic awareness, phonics/decoding, reading fluency, vocabulary, and comprehension are the five essential elements of effective reading programs identified by the NRP. We strongly agree with the findings of the panel—these elements must be taught to students in their reading program.

Rather than getting into in-depth detail on research and theory related to these topics, our intent in this series is to provide you with a collection of simple, practical, and relatively easy-to-implement instructional strategies, proven through research and actual practice, for teaching. In this book we consider excellent literacy instruction in the context of providing culturally responsive support for students.

Professional Development in Literacy

Effective literacy instruction requires teachers to be knowledgeable, informed professionals capable of assessing student needs and responding to those needs with an assortment of instructional strategies. Whether you are new to the field or a classroom veteran, ongoing professional development is imperative. Professional development influences instructional practices, which, in turn, affect student achievement (Wenglinsky, 2000). Effective professional development is not simply an isolated program or activity; rather, it is an ongoing, consistent learning effort where links between theoretical knowledge and the application of that knowledge to daily classroom practices are forged in consistent and meaningful ways (Renyi, 1998).

Researchers have noted several characteristics of effective professional development: It must be grounded in research-based practices; it must be collaborative, allowing teachers ample opportunities to share knowledge, as well as teaching and learning challenges, among colleagues; and it must actively engage teachers in assessing, observing, and responding to the learning and development of their students (Darling-Hammond & McLaughlin, 1995). This professional development series, *Evidence-Based Instruction in Reading: A Professional Development Guide*, is intended to provide a road map for systematic, participatory professional development initiatives.

Using the Books

Each of the first five books in the *Evidence-Based Instruction* series addresses one major component of literacy instruction identified by the National Reading Panel (2000) and widely accepted in the field as necessary for effective literacy programs: phonemic awareness, phonics, fluency, vocabulary, and comprehension. These five components are not, by any means, the only components needed for effective literacy instruction. Access to appropriate reading materials, productive home–school connections, and a desire to learn to read and write are also critical pieces of the literacy puzzle. Moreover, effective instruction for struggling readers using Response to Intervention (Wisniewski, Padak, & Rasinski, 2011) and instruction that is culturally sensitive—the focus of this book—are critically important issues. It is our hope that by focusing in depth on major literacy components, we can provide educators and professional development facilitators with concrete guidelines and suggestions for enhancing literacy instruction for all students.

Each book is intended to be used by professional development facilitators, be they administrators, literacy coaches, reading specialists, and/or classroom teachers, and by program participants as they engage in professional development initiatives or in-service programs within schools or school districts. The use of the series can be adapted to meet the specific needs and goals of a group of educators. For example, a school may choose to hold a series of professional development sessions on each of the five major components of literacy instruction; it may choose to focus in depth on one or two components that are most relevant to their literacy program; or it may choose to focus on specific aspects, such as assessment or instructional strategies, of one or more of the areas. The books may also be useful in professional book club settings. (An icon is included at spots for book club discussion.) It is important that, in collaboration with teachers, professional development needs be carefully assessed so that the appropriate content can be selected to meet those needs.

Introduction

Culturally Responsive Instruction

*B*arely a week before the school year was to begin, Salome entered the United States as a 6-year-old adoptee from El Salvador. Until the day she walked into the airport with her new parents, Salome had never seen a magic toilet flush itself; had never drunk sweetness through a long, skinny tube; and certainly had never heard a voice from out of nowhere wafting through the air.

A week later when she stepped into Mrs. Fawcett's first-grade class, she smiled and proudly said one of the few English phrases she knew: "Good morning." Then she mimicked a TV fast-food commercial, which she didn't understand: "Where's the beef?" Mrs. Fawcett knew next to nothing about El Salvador. Although she knew it was in South America, she couldn't locate it on a map. She knew no Spanish, nothing about Salome's birth family, and very little about the political unrest that led to Salome's adoption. What Mrs. Fawcett did know was that it was the first day of first grade and she had to begin teaching Salome to read, along with 23 other 6-year-olds. Salome did pretty well in first grade, though it's hard to say who learned more that year—Salome or her teacher!

No doubt you clearly remember the first English language learner (ELL) who entered your classroom. Were you worried? Did you seek out the advice of colleagues or ask your principal for help? Perhaps your teaching journey has led you to an area where poverty is the norm. Do you wrestle with how to negotiate the lack of educational experiences your students have had? Do you find yourself wondering how to teach children with hungry bellies? Or maybe you've spent your career as a teacher in a school with a high population of students whose minority status you do not share. Do you struggle to understand what motivates them? Do you anguish over a perceived lack of parental involvement?

xviii
....

INTRODUCTION

*Culturally
Responsive
Instruction*

This book is for teachers who answered *yes* to any of those questions. It is for teachers whose ELL numbers have steadily increased. It is for teachers who teach in inner cities and teachers who teach in poor rural areas. It is for teachers who teach children from cultures different from their own. In short, it is for every teacher because, if you have not experienced cultural diversity in your classroom yet, a look at U.S. population projections will show you that you don't have long to wait (see U.S. Population Projections, 2005–2050 in Chapter 1).

This book is modest in scope when compared with the complexity of diversity in our schools. We know we cannot answer all your questions about teaching reading to culturally diverse students. We hope, though, you will gain insight into the premises that support culturally responsive reading instruction and that you will add some instructional strategies to your repertoire from among the evidence-based ideas you will find here. Most importantly, we hope this book becomes a springboard to conversations you have with colleagues because that's where the best answers will be found.

Chapter 1 begins by placing culturally responsive instruction (CRI) within the context of the rapidly changing demographics of our public schools. The definition of CRI that follows this discussion includes various components identified by experts in the field. A brief summary of current research and professional literature on CRI is included; additional research is woven throughout the remaining chapters. Chapter 1 ends with an invitation to analyze, clarify, extend, discuss, and apply the information presented in the chapter.

Chapter 2 begins with the "Big Ideas" of assessment within the context of *backward design*—that is, pre-assess to determine what students need, determine acceptable evidence, and then plan learning experiences and instruction. In this chapter, you will find a number of practical strategies for assessing students' cultures, vocabulary, and comprehension; your own instruction; and your school's readiness to address cultural diversity. At the end of this chapter, you are invited to self-evaluate your instruction.

Chapter 3 begins with a look at what a number of researchers found when they studied classrooms where effective literacy instruction for diverse students was taking place. Then we present guidelines, based on these findings, for planning your literacy instruction. This chapter includes many instructional strategies you can use for vocabulary and comprehension development as well as strategies for getting students actively participating in the lessons. At the end of the chapter, you are invited to discuss the strategies and consider which ones you would like to use in your classroom.

xix
....

INTRODUCTION
*Culturally
Responsive
Instruction*

Chapter 4 covers issues that are becoming increasingly important in today's classrooms: English language learners, Latino/a students, and students with special education needs. In addition, we share some ideas on incorporating new literacies (e.g., technology-based learning) into the culturally responsive classroom. Discussion questions at the end of the chapter provide you the opportunity to discuss these important issues with your colleagues and to plan instruction based on what you learned.

Chapter 5 provides you with resources—including professional books and web resources—for implementing culturally responsive reading instruction at the classroom and school levels.

Throughout the book, you will find ample room to make notes, jot down insights, and record questions about various aspects of planning and implementing effective CRI. We encourage you to use these spaces to record reactions, insights, and ideas that are particularly relevant to your own students and their families. You will find these notes invaluable as you begin to develop your own concrete plan to make CRI more effective for all your students.

Culturally Responsive Instruction: Definitions, Research, and Considerations

CHAPTER 1

*Culturally
Responsive
Instruction:
Definitions,
Research, and
Considerations*

*T*here's a good chance that most of you reading this book are white and middle class; more than half of you are likely female. We make those assumptions based on the following facts: 83.5% of teachers in the United States are white, 58% of them are female, and their average salary is $49,600 (U.S. Department of Education, 2009).

At the same time, only 61.8% of students are white, 16% are black, 16.7% are Hispanic, 1.3% are American Indian/Alaska Native, and 4% are Asian/Pacific Islander. One student in five is likely to be an English language learner (ELL) (Richard-Amato & Snow, 2005). Nearly half of all students (42.9%) receive free or reduced-price lunches (U.S. Department of Education, 2009). The poverty rate is actually higher than that because older students are more reluctant to report the need for a free or reduced-price lunch. Furthermore, diversity in the United States is increasing each year. While the impact currently is greatest in urban areas, rural and suburban schools are becoming more and more diverse and will be even more so in the near future. Consider what your future classroom might be like based on the projections in Table 1.1 (Passel & Cohn, 2008).

Book Club

Table 1.1
U.S. Population Projections, 2005–2050

Share of Total Population	2005	2050
Foreign born	12%	19%
White	67%	47%
Hispanic	14%	29%
Black	13%	13%
Asian	5%	9%

So, whether you are in the majority of teachers (83% white) or in the minority (6.9% black, 6.6% Hispanic, and 1.5% Asian/Pacific Islander) (U.S. Department of Education, 2009), it is essential that you plan instruction that is responsive to the cultures represented in your classroom.

What Is Culturally Responsive Instruction?

3

CHAPTER 1

*Culturally
Responsive
Instruction:
Definitions,
Research, and
Considerations*

For this book, we define *culturally responsive instruction* (CRI) as using knowledge of student cultures and modalities to select and apply strategies and resources for instruction, while engaging in self-reflection. There are five components to this definition, which can be divided into two parts: the *teaching* and the *teacher*. The first part, the *teaching*, contains four coherent puzzle pieces: (1) instructional strategies, (2) multiple texts, (3) student cultures, and (4) multiple modalities. The second part is the *teacher*, who engages in reflection about self—that is, who examines his or her own culture, perspectives, and biases. In CRI, it is essential that the teacher self-reflect in these ways, while engaging in teaching that focuses on understanding student cultures (e.g., hooks, 1994; Nieto, 2010; Robins, Lindsey, Lindsey, & Terrell, 2005; Sleeter, 2005). Together, the *teaching* and the *teacher* make up the big picture of CRI. Figure 1.1 shows the teaching and the teacher in a concrete

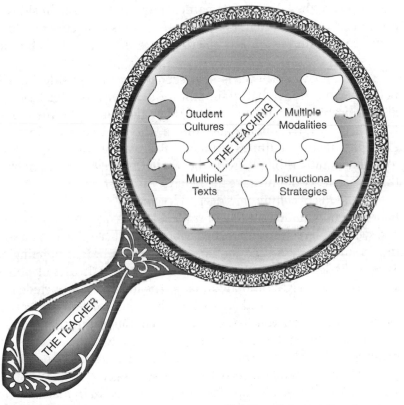

Figure 1.1 Culturally Responsive Instruction Is a Coherent Puzzle of Teaching Components and a Mirror for Teacher Self-Reflection

4
....

CHAPTER 1

*Culturally
Responsive
Instruction:
Definitions,
Research, and
Considerations*

image, where the four puzzle pieces make up the teaching and the mirror represents the self-reflection of the teacher.

Culture, then, is the heart of CRI. What comes to mind when you hear the term *culture*? Most likely, culture brings to mind a particular group of people, but other thoughts may come to mind as well, like beliefs, values, and behaviors shared within a particular societal system. Nieto (2010) notes that "culture is complex and intricate; it cannot be reduced to holidays, foods or dances, although these of course are elements of culture" (p. 9). Although Nieto affirms these as elements of culture, such items as holidays, foods, or dances are commonly thought of as a surface level of culture—what Hidalgo (1993) calls the *concrete* level, which is at the surface of the three levels of culture: concrete, behavioral, and symbolic.

This surface or concrete level contains examples of what we see when we look at another culture from the outside in. Many times we tend to make a judgment—we look at a group of people, see the clothes they wear or their particular physical characteristics as different from ourselves, and label them. This judgment can lead to a stereotype, or the labeling of a particular group by those outside the group based on prejudgments or assumptions. The concrete level may also contain the artifacts of a culture, which can be seen but not understood (Schein, 1992).

The behavioral level is also seen from the outside in. The behaviors, like nonverbal communication, are visible. This level can also be problematic because of the judgments made and the stereotypes held by those outside the culture who observe behaviors. For example, in some cultures students, as a way of showing respect, look down, rather than looking the teacher in the eye. Not knowing this, a teacher could mistake the behavior for disrespect.

Thinking of culture at its deepest level, the symbolic level, can enhance teachers' understanding of student knowledge and experiences. The symbolic level informs the behaviors and artifacts that can be seen in a culture. For example, suppose a student is not completing an assigned independent reading task (behavior) and dresses like other students in her neighborhood (artifact). The teacher can conclude that she does not care to read. But when the behavior and artifact are viewed from the symbolic level, the judgment can be turned into questions: Might she not be interested in the text? Or does she have trouble reading the words? Or could she lack the background knowledge needed to understand the text? These questions get to the heart of the student's knowledge and experiences in order to assist in matching her interest and skills with an individual reading selection. The symbolic level, then, is the level most central to a culture, and teachers can get to this level when they seek the perspectives of their students by asking questions and finding out what they see, hear, feel, and think.

A definition of culture that focuses on the perspective of those in the cultural group is offered by Banks (2004). According to Banks, culture contains six elements: (1) values and behavioral styles; (2) language and dialects; (3) nonverbal communications; (4) cultural cognitiveness; (5) perspectives, worldviews, and frames of reference; and (6) identification. Noteworthy in this definition is the word *perspectives*. Culture is neither what we see about students nor what we assume they think. Rather, it is a point of view that guides what students do. Therefore, students' perspectives are what we need to *respond to* in our instruction. We need to know their cultural perspectives—their knowledge, experiences, and methods of communicating—in order to meet their individual reading needs.

If culture refers to students' points of view, what about the term *diversity*? Au (2004) uses the term to refer to "students who differ from the mainstream" with respect to ethnicity, primary language, and social class. In the United States, these students often are African American, Asian American, Latino, or Native American in ethnicity; speak home languages other than English; and come from poor or working-class families (p. 392).

In this book, we will use Au's definition of diversity, recognizing that "students who differ from the mainstream" include children not specifically mentioned by Au but who would be included in her definition—children of various ethnic or religious groups, immigrants, second generation U.S. citizens, Native Alaskan children, children from rural Appalachia—in short, any group who "brings cultural knowledge, prior experiences, and performance styles" (Gay, 2000, p. 29) that diverge from the way we have traditionally done school in the United States. We will examine instruction for those diverse groups in the context of Banks' definition of culture. Although the suggestions we make apply to English Language Learners (ELLs), we will also address that population specifically in Chapter 4 because they make up such a large segment of our diverse student population.

Is Culturally Responsive Instruction Just a New Name for Multicultural Education?

Multicultural education is a field of study or an umbrella that captures five dimensions that need teachers' attention (Banks, 1995): content integration, the knowledge construction process, prejudice

5

CHAPTER 1
*Culturally
Responsive
Instruction:
Definitions,
Research, and
Considerations*

6
....

CHAPTER 1

*Culturally
Responsive
Instruction:
Definitions,
Research, and
Considerations*

reduction, an equity pedagogy, and an empowering school culture and social structure. CRI focuses on each of these areas and is a foundation for instruction under the multicultural education umbrella, rather than an add-on.

Historically, multicultural education has been seen as "an activity that happens at a set period of the day [or] another subject to be covered" (Nieto, 2010, p. 75). In this view, diversity is a supplement to the regular curriculum—for example, including in the social studies curriculum a unit on Mexico or introducing notable African American leaders during Black History Month. The rest of the curriculum focuses on mainstream historians and events, where students do not gain experience with cultural inequalities or how cultures are interconnected (Banks, 1997; Nieto, 1996, 1999; Sleeter & Grant, 2009). This type of multicultural education focuses on celebrating differences in shallow ways (Nieto, 2010).

CRI, on the other hand, aims to reflect the ideals of democracy in a diverse society using Banks' five dimensions of multicultural education. It allows students to see from several cultural and ethnic perspectives and is engaging for students and diverse in its teaching and learning dimensions (Sleeter, 2005). In reading instruction, such an approach enables culture, language, and literacy to intersect (Nieto, 2010).

What Does the Research Say About Culturally Responsive Instruction?

Like all human beings, culturally diverse students need to belong (Maslow, 1970). Research has shown that, when cultural differences are ignored in classrooms, diverse students feel a heightened sense of alienation (Greene & Abt-Perkins, 2003; Igoa, 1995; Schmidt, 1998, 2002). Frequently, they feel they must abandon their cultural background in order to assimilate into the majority culture. This dissonance has been linked to poor literacy development and high dropout rates (Edwards, 2004; Edwards, Pleasants, & Franklin, 1999; Nieto, 1999; Payne, DeVol, & Smith, 2000; Schmidt, 1998, 1999).

However, when teachers honor what students already know and celebrate who they are as individuals and as members of a cultural group, students achieve at higher levels (Gay, 2000; Tatum, 2000). Research indicates that in addition to obtaining higher grades and standardized test scores, students exhibit better interpersonal skills, a better understanding of interconnections among individuals and cultures, and an appreciation for the social nature of learning (Chapman, 1994; Foster, 1995; Hollins, 1996; Hollins, King, & Hayman, 1994; Ladson-Billings, 1994, 1995a, 1995b). As you proceed through the chapters in this book, you will encounter more research in support of CRI. In short, decades of research point to the benefits of CRI. So how do you get there?

How Can You Be Culturally Responsive?

The first step to becoming culturally responsive is to pay attention to the symbolic or deep level of culture. This means accepting that the cultures of some of your students are different from your culture without imposing a value judgment of "good" or "bad." Indeed, getting to know students is a priority in the classroom. However, when faced with a student who has no books or magazines in the home, can you recognize the family's literacy materials—U.S. mail, bus schedules, church bulletins, and mail-order catalogues— as different from those in your culture but not good or bad? When parents do not come for parent conferences, can you accept as different from your culture, but not good or bad, the fact that in some Latino communities parents consider it an insult to the teacher if they try to teach their own child? When children interrupt in class, can you respect as different from your culture, but not good or bad, the fact that in some cultures children are encouraged to "chime in"?

Attention to the symbolic level of culture cannot happen unless teachers study issues of diversity and engage in self-reflection. In fact, multicultural researchers and educators have long pointed out the need for teachers' self-examination of value judgments. In her well-known text *Teaching to Transgress: Education as the Practice of Freedom*, hooks (1994) points out that "the unwillingness to approach teaching from a standpoint that includes awareness of race, sex, and class is often rooted in the fear that classrooms will be uncontrollable, that emotions and passions will not be controlled" (p. 39). Although your involvement in this book shows your willingness to engage in and dedication to cultural responsiveness, your continuous awareness of fears, judgments, and even biases that emerge from your own background and experiences will enhance your implementation of CRI in the classroom. Only after such honest soul-searching will you truly be ready to plan concrete ways of

8

CHAPTER 1

*Culturally
Responsive
Instruction:
Definitions,
Research, and
Considerations*

meeting the literacy needs of your diverse students. Here are three ways to begin this searching:

1. *Examine your own culture.* What is your culture? Thinking about "culture" may bring many words to mind—for example, *religion, ethnicity, race, clothing, gender, foods, time,* and *language.* Expand this list, and then categorize the words according to the three levels of culture described above (i.e., concrete, behavioral, and symbolic). Choose five to eight words from this list that are most important to who you are. What do you notice about this list? What surprises you about this list? Take the list a step further, and draw a circle. Divide the circle into the number of pieces that corresponds to the number of words you chose. Decide the size of each piece based on how important that aspect of culture is to your life. What do you notice about the sizes of the pieces?

Book Club

2. *Enhance your skill in seeing multiple perspectives.* How do you think? What do you see? What do you feel? What do you do? Ask these questions of another person like a student in your class. How does the student think? What does the student see? What does the student feel? What does the student do? Then compare this perspective with your own, and add other perspectives to your comparisons. How is each student's perspective similar to or different from yours—perhaps as a teacher, as an adult, or even as a student when you were this student's age? How is this student's perspective different from that of another student?

3. *Explore your connections with multicultural terms.* Common multicultural terms include words like *prejudice, discrimination,* and *stereotype.* Review what each of these terms means below. Then ask yourself these questions: In what ways have I been prejudiced? In what ways might I have discriminated against others? In what ways might I have stereotyped others? In what ways have I changed, or could I change, prejudice, discrimination, or stereotypes?

   • *Prejudice:* A thought that is a conclusion about a person. It is a judgment that is made before gathering information about the background and experiences of an individual.
   • *Discrimination:* A behavior that follows a particular conclusion (i.e., prejudice) about an individual or group.
   • *Stereotype:* A label placed on an individual or group due to a particular conclusion (e.g., prejudice) about that individual or group.

Continuous awareness of your own fears, judgments, and even biases is a necessity for CRI, and recognizing other cultures as being different from your own, but not good or bad, can be tricky at times. Recognizing *instruction* as good or bad for culturally diverse students is a bit easier because of the research that supports it. The following questions may help you assess the extent to which you are planning CRI:

9

CHAPTER 1
*Culturally
Responsive
Instruction:
Definitions,
Research, and
Considerations*

1. How do you assess student cultures so that you can make appropriate instructional decisions?
2. How do you apply reading strategies that focus on connection to cultures?
3. Do you attend to the learning modalities of your students?
4. Do you use materials that are multicultural—that is, ones that reflect the backgrounds and experiences of diverse students?
5. Do you use materials that are multitextual—that is, ones that are in multiple formats like print, visual, audio, and interactive?
6. How do you motivate your students?
7. How do you address the elements of effective reading instruction (phonemic awareness, phonics, fluency, vocabulary, and comprehension)?

Book Club

Conclusion

In the chapters that follow, we will provide suggestions for assessing your diverse learners and share instructional strategies that have been shown by research to be effective for this population. As you move forward with this topic, you might do well to keep in mind some of the traits Whitaker (2004) listed in *What Great Teachers Do Differently*:

- Great teachers have high expectations for students but even higher expectations for themselves.
- Great teachers know who the variable is in the classroom: *They are.*
- Great teachers consistently strive to improve, and they focus on something they can control—their own performance (p. 127).

In the end, what really matters for your culturally diverse learners is YOU!

Professional Development

ACED: Analysis, Clarification, Extension, Discussion

I. REFLECTION (10–15 minutes)

ANALYSIS

- What, for you, were the most interesting and/or important ideas in this chapter?

_____

_____

_____

_____

- What information was new to you or different from your own prior perceptions of culture, diversity, or CRI?

_____

_____

_____

_____

CLARIFICATION

- Did anything surprise you? Confuse you? Cause you to "squirm" a bit?

_____

_____

_____

_____

EXTENSION

- What additional questions do you have about CRI?

_____

_____

_____

_____

- Describe one unforgettable classroom experience with a culturally diverse student.

  _____

  _____

  _____

  _____

- Describe your own culture from the concrete, behavior, and symbolic levels.

  _____

  _____

  _____

  _____

- Do you have any new insights about the cultural context of literacy?

  _____

  _____

  _____

  _____

- How might the information presented in this chapter be applied in your own teaching situation?

  _____

  _____

  _____

  _____

II. DISCUSSION (30 minutes)

- Form groups of 4–6 members.
- Appoint a *facilitator (timer)* and *recorder.*
- Share responses. Make sure that each person has shared his or her responses to each category (Analysis/Clarification/Extension).
- Help each other with any areas of confusion.
- Answer and/or discuss questions raised by group members.
- On chart paper, the recorder should summarize the main discussion points and identify issues or questions the group would like to raise for general discussion.

12

CHAPTER 1

*Culturally
Responsive
Instruction:
Definitions,
Research, and
Considerations*

III. APPLICATION (10 minutes)

• Have your students create portfolios that include examples of their cultures. What might they include? How can you use what you learn from their portfolios?

_____

_____

_____

_____

• Based on your reflection and discussion, how might you apply what you have learned about CRI?

_____

_____

_____

_____

Assessing Reading Instruction for Cultural Responsiveness

*S*uzanne teaches fifth grade in a suburb east of Cleveland, Ohio. For the first 22 years of her career, the district was considered upper middle class, with a solid school tax base and high student achievement overall. Then things began to change. Suzanne explained:

> It wasn't gradual. It seemed to happen overnight. Families started migrating eastward from the inner city. Not only did that mean more students from lower-income families, but also it meant more students with English as their second language. The first year that some of our subgroups did not meet No Child Left Behind requirements, we knew we had to do things differently.

Suzanne's superintendent brought in a nationally known speaker for a three-part series on teaching children of poverty. He sent teachers to workshops focused on English language learners (ELLs), and he purchased books on culturally responsive instruction (CRI) for teachers' after-school book clubs. The following fall Suzanne was ready—or so she thought. She had read voraciously, attended every professional development opportunity offered, and spent long hours in the summer preparing lessons to address cultural diversity. Her heart was in the right place; her lesson plans were written; her materials were gathered. Unfortunately, Suzanne had sidestepped a most important principle: You have to know your students before you can plan instruction for them.

In years past (and unfortunately in some classrooms still), teachers planned instruction in the following sequence: (1) Determine lesson objectives, (2) plan activities to teach the objectives, (3) gather materials, (4) teach, and (5) assess. Wiggins and McTighe (2005) propose that we begin with the last step instead—that we assess students first so that we know what objectives, activities, and materials they need. The three-step planning process Wiggins and McTighe advocate, known as *backward design*, involves these steps: (1) Identify desired results, which you will determine through pre-assessment; (2) determine acceptable evidence; and (3) plan learning experiences and instruction.

In the spirit of backward design, we have placed the assessment chapter before the strategies chapter in this book. In this chapter, we will provide strategies for getting to know your students' and their families' cultures, literacy histories, and learning needs; assessing various aspects of your classroom instruction; and assessing whether the school as a whole is situated for addressing the reading needs of diverse learners. Then, in Chapter 3 we will share instructional strategies you can use, once you know what your students need.

Big Ideas of Assessment

In each of the books in this series, we have identified several "big ideas" to guide your thinking about assessment. These big ideas apply to assessing all aspects of literacy learning (indeed, to all learning), but the comments and examples below frame them in the context of CRI.

• *Focus on critical information.* Aim for a direct connection between the assessment tools/strategies you use and what you need to know. You can identify the critical information you need to know by considering the broad definitions of culture, diversity, and CRI presented in Chapter 1 with your own students in mind. You may also find other books in this series to be helpful in determining broad definitions for phonemic awareness, phonics, fluency, vocabulary, and comprehension.

So, for example, if you determine that information about a student's home culture is critical, you might use the cultural interview approach discussed in this chapter and read some books related to that child's culture. If you decide that you need to know more about an ELL's level of social vocabulary, you might look for situations where the student is talking with peers, rather than just observing teacher–student interactions. If, on the other hand, you need to know about that child's level of academic vocabulary, you might want to use some of the vocabulary assessments suggested in this chapter.

• *Look for patterns of behavior.* Tierney (1998) notes that assessment "should be viewed as ongoing and suggestive, rather than fixed or definitive" (p. 385). Think of the ongoing process of looking for behavior patterns in two steps: first, collecting the information and, second, documenting the information. Collecting the information can involve several methods. Among the more common are observing and interviewing—that is, watching for behavior and asking children directed questions that they answer orally. Common ways to document the information are anecdotally (i.e., in written notes) and in a checklist.

For example, while observing an ELL during silent reading, you notice that she skips pages. But the next day you notice that she is not skipping pages. In a one-to-one oral interview, you ask her to describe people, places, or events of the two stories she read during silent reading. She describes the people and places in one of the stories and the events in neither story, and you follow up with prompts

16
....
CHAPTER 2

*Assessing Reading
Instruction for
Cultural
Responsiveness*

about particular vocabulary associated with the people and places. You then create an entry in your notes regarding which books she had read and perhaps note on your checklist which questions she answered. Over time, you will be able to discern patterns that answer such questions as these: Is she interested in the text? What vocabulary does she know? How does she comprehend while reading silently?

These questions address the student's culture—her background knowledge and experiences—and how successfully she is able to apply knowledge and experiences to the process of comprehending what she reads. It would be impossible for us to address every culture you might encounter in your classroom. Therefore, you should carefully document the data that you collect through methods that are formal and informal so that you can look for patterns that will help you understand each child's needs.

• *Recognize developmental progressions [can't, can sometimes, can always] and children's cultural or linguistic differences.* Tierney (1998) advises that assessment "should be more developmental and sustained than piecemeal and shortsighted" (p. 384). It should "build upon, recognize, and value rather than displace what students have experienced in their worlds" (p. 381). For example, research overwhelmingly supports the practice of using the child's first language to accelerate English acquisition (Greene, 1999; Krashen, 1996; Krashen & McField, 2005; Oller & Eilers, 2002). Doing so provides schemas in the first language so that English is more comprehensible. Applying this principle to literacy, starting with students' reading strengths in the home language allows them to "bootstrap" into English literacy (Genesee, 2005).

Children of poverty will have different language needs than do ELLs. Sussman (2009) calls these children "Kids from Chaos" because of the turmoil that may reign in their homes due to unemployment, substance abuse, or a myriad of other social factors. These children often lack the basic necessities such as food, clothing, and nurturance. Perhaps more significantly, they lack substantive relationships with responsible peers and adults. Because these children often lack appropriate oral language skills to connect to and negotiate with others or to express themselves, they may exhibit behavior problems or depression, lack time-management skills, and struggle academically. Lectures or teacher-talk are usually lost on kids from chaos because they lack a sufficient academic vocabulary to easily process information.

As you can see from these two examples, determining a student's developmental progress will always be intertwined with the cultural context.

- *Be parsimonious.* The question: How much assessment information do you need? The answer: only enough to help you make good instructional decisions. Simply put, if the student continues to struggle after you have assessed him or her and carried out subsequent instructional plans, then you probably need more information. One way to conceptualize the quantity of information needed is to think in terms of three layers of assessment information, as shown in Figure 2.1 (Rasinski, Padak, & Fawcett, 2010).

Begin with a broad plan to assess all students' reading at the beginning of the year and then perhaps quarterly. After each assessment cycle concludes, think about results: What [or who] do you still have questions about? This is the point where you move to the second layer of the triangle. Here, you will do more targeted (and time-consuming) reading assessments. You might work individually with a student, perhaps doing more of what you've already done or using a more comprehensive assessment.

For example, once you have assessed all students and have further questions about an ELL, you might assess that student's comprehension by using picture cues for a story retelling. Or you might assess comprehension with a different text and with words at another grade level. This more focused assessment in the second layer of the triangle is also related to the Response to Intervention (RTI) model for which there is a separate text in this series (Wisniewski, Padak, &

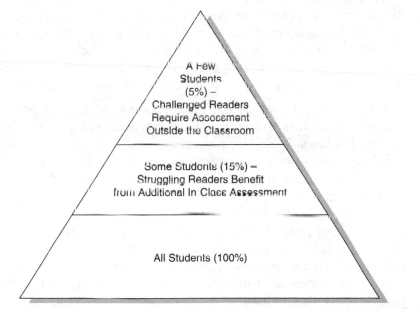

A Few
Students
(5%) –
Challenged Readers
Require Assessment
Outside the Classroom

Some Students (15%) –
Struggling Readers Benefit
from Additional In-Class Assessment

All Students (100%)

Figure 2.1 A Model for Classroom Assessment

Rasinski, 2011). In RTI, Tier 1 assessments (the bottom layer of the triangle in Figure 2.1) are for all students. Tier 2 is targeted for students for whom you need more information. Tier 3 is reserved for students with the most need for more assessment information. If you still have questions after Tier 2 assessment, don't hesitate to ask for outside help. A student or two in the class may benefit from a diagnosis by a reading specialist or other highly specialized professional. Don't delay. Every lost day represents lost opportunities for that student's learning. Above all, keep assessments at these different layers related to one another, focused on the same key reading issues.

• *Use instructional situations for assessment purposes.* Tierney (1998) notes that ideally "[a]ssessments should emerge from the classroom rather than be imposed upon it" (p. 375). We can think of two good reasons for this stance, one conceptual and the other practical. From a conceptual perspective, you want to know how students behave in typical instructional situations. After all, a major purpose of assessment is to provide instructional guidance. And practically, gathering assessment information from instruction saves time for your teaching and students' learning. Students don't learn much of value during testing sessions.

Much can be learned by simply listening. For example, paying close attention as students of diverse backgrounds talk about a story can provide significant information about their background knowledge. Listening to ELLs talk with their peers on the playground or in the cafeteria can provide information you cannot get by listening to them talk in classroom discussions. Taking note of words used in a student's writing can give you insight into his or her vocabulary development. Above all, take West's (1998) advice to heart: "I want instruction and evaluation to be in meaningful authentic contexts" (p. 550).

• *Include plans for (a) using assessment information to guide instruction and (b) sharing assessment information with students and their parents.* The last step of your assessment planning might be to double-check ideas against their primary purposes: to help you teach more effectively and to communicate your insights to students and their parents. With regard to the former, it may be particularly important to think about how you can adjust instruction for students from diverse backgrounds. How can you match instruction better to the student's background knowledge and experiences? What texts might you use that would reflect your students' cultures and, thus, create interest in reading? What kind of participation might provide opportunities for students to talk about the text in order to improve vocabulary learning?

Moreover, consider how you can share information about reading with students and their parents. Knowing that they are making progress will keep students engaged in their learning. Assessment conversations are also good ways to help students develop more abstract concepts about reading. Remember that CRI extends to the family as well. When communicating with parents of culturally diverse students, it is important to understand the social structure of the family in that particular culture. In Chapter 1, we talked about the fact that not all cultures respond to parental involvement in education as teachers sometimes expect, but it doesn't mean the parents don't care. In the pages that follow, we provide some suggestions for getting to know about the child's home culture. Tierney (1998) reminds us that it's important to keep parents not only informed but also, more than that, involved. This can be a challenge with parents who do not speak English, parents who are working several jobs just to make ends meet, or parents who feel it is not their place to teach their child. However, "[r]ather than keep the parent or caregiver at arm's length. . . , we need to embrace the concerns that parents have and the contributions they can make" (p. 380).

The assessment strategies in this chapter are divided into four sections: (1) assessing student cultures, (2) assessing reading skills (vocabulary and comprehension), (3) assessing your instruction, and (4) assessing your school's readiness for culturally responsive instruction. These sections are in no particular order. Determine an area where you are lacking information and start there.

Assessing Student Cultures

Meyer (2000) uses the term *culture load* to refer to the way language and culture are related and the amount of cultural knowledge required to comprehend meaning or to participate in an activity. Culture load includes how teachers expect interaction to occur in a classroom— when to speak, when to stay silent, when to raise hands, and when to write. Such expectations vary from one culture to the next. Culturally diverse students do not acquire these classroom behavioral norms independently; they must be taught. This requires a conscious knowledge of students' cultures and the classroom culture so that a plan can be made for bridging the two.

The best way to get to know your students' cultures is to embed your inquiry into everyday instruction and learning activities. Talk with them in the classroom. Play with them on the playground.

Observe them working and playing with others. Invite family members in to share aspects of their culture with your class. Most importantly, never assume.

A cultural interview with your students and their parents can help you gather information and simultaneously build trust and rapport. The purpose of your interview is to gain information about a school-aged student's likes and dislikes in school and/or out of school within the student's current culture. This knowledge informs your use of the culture and experiences of different ethnic groups as a launch pad to teach more effectively (Gay, 2000).

The cultural interview in Appendix B provides a list of questions within multiple categories: reading, computer use, music, games, and other activities. These categories reflect different types of texts that 21st century children and adolescents use outside of school. For example, in its report released in January 2010 on the media use for youth from ages 8 to 18 (Rideout, Foehr, & Roberts, 2010), the Kaiser Family Foundation reported an average 38 minutes spent a day on print, as compared to an average of four and a half hours with television content, two and a half hours with music and audio content, and one and a half hours with the computer. The averages for television, music, computer time, and video games increased from 2004 to 2009. Because of this increase, selecting from the questions in Appendix B will not only ascertain student interests that enable you to be responsive with instruction but also provide information that enables you to respond to student cultures using multiple texts.

Conducting the interview involves several steps that are based on the time you have available, the relationship you already have built with the student or group of students you will interview, and the information you want to know. We suggest the following steps while planning the interview.

Step 1 *Decide whom you will interview and why.* You may want to choose your whole class and divide them in groups. Or you may select a student who is particularly quiet, is new to the classroom, is not participating as you had expected, or seems to have difficulties with the learning tasks in your classroom.

Step 2 *Determine the purpose of your interview.* The general purpose of this interview is to gain more information about students' backgrounds and experiences in order to inform teaching practice in a diversity context. Is there a specific lesson, unit, or literacy center that you have in mind when conducting the interview?

Step 3 *Obtain informal permission for your interview.* Permission is based on the purpose of your interview. When the purpose is to inform teaching practice, the interview includes questions that you would normally ask as you get to know students within the scope of your professional role. Permission, then, becomes a matter of respect for the student. Ask something like "May I have permission to ask you questions about your interests?"

Step 4 *Choose interview questions.* Read through the interview samples, select appropriate questions and edit them, and/or develop your own questions based upon what you would normally ask within the scope of your teaching.

Step 5 *Determine the setting and materials for the interview.* Choose a place that will be comfortable for the interviewee. Materials for the interview may include a laptop if you are typing the answers or a pen/pencil if you are writing them. Have notes if you need them as well.

Step 6 *Conduct the interview. Include an introduction and a closure.* Decide what you will say when introducing the interview to set the tone. This may include a restatement of the purpose of the interview as well as an introduction statement. An opening might be: "Have you ever been interviewed before?" or "I will ask you several questions about your interests inside and outside of school. Ready?" Make sure the student understands that you will not be "grading" his or her answers. During the interview, keep in mind prompts like "Tell me more about that," "What do you mean by . . .?" and other clarifying questions offered within the interview in Appendix B. Repeating what your student says also helps to either clarify a response or encourage an extended response. Select a closure appropriate to your relationship with the student, such as "Thank you" or "Anything you would like to ask me?" Selecting information that you learned about the student ("I especially liked your comments about. . .") or a strength that you noticed helps to solidify your relationship, while also transitioning from the interview to the next task.

Notice that the interview addresses interests based on what the child does. Understanding home behaviors gives information on the symbolic or deep level of culture that we introduced in Chapter 1. In addition to gathering information from students themselves, you can expand your cultural assessment to the greater community where your students live. Observations made by walking through the community and visiting the local library and merchants can provide information about what your students see every day outside of the school that you can also use in your curriculum. The following interview questions (Sleeter, 2005) can be posed not only to the families of your students, but also to others who live in the community:

- What are the main assets of the community?
- What are people in the community especially good at?
- Describe how you would like this community to be 10 years from now.
- What does this community have going for it that will help reach that goal?
- What are the main barriers to reaching that goal? What is the community doing to address those barriers?
- What needs does the community have?
- As a teacher, how can I best serve this community?

Another excellent way to become familiar with the cultures of your students begins with a trip to your favorite bookstore or public library. There are novels, both contemporary and historical, and true stories that will satisfy your desire to read for pleasure and at the same time give you insight into your students' cultures. For example, the book *Among Schoolchildren*, Tracy Kidder's (1990) haunting account of the inner-city life of two young boys, will give you insight into children of poverty. In *Ordinary Resurrections*, Jonathan Kozol (2001) gives us a look at schoolchildren of South Bronx's most dismal neighborhood, Mott Haven. *Three Cups of Tea*, a *New York Times* bestseller by Greg Mortenson and David Oliver Relin (2007), is a captivating story about life in Pakistan and Afghanistan.

Be sure to read Shirley Brice Heath's classic studies of language learning in two culturally different communities only a few miles apart in the southeastern United States (Heath, 1983, 1994). Heath lived among families in "Roadville," a white working-class community steeped for four generations in the life of the textile mills, and "Trackton," a black working-class community whose older generations grew up farming but whose younger generations worked in the textile mills.

In tracing the children's language development, Heath found deep cultural differences between the two communities and the teachers who taught the children. One example among many in the book *Ways with Words* tells how babies in the two communities learn to talk. In Trackton,

[c]hildren do not expect adults to ask them questions, for in Trackton children are not seen as information-givers or question-answerers. This is especially true of questions for which adults already have an answer. Because adults do not consider children appropriate conversational partners to the exclusion of other people who are around, they do not construct questions especially for children, nor do they use questions to give the young an opportunity to show off their knowledge about the world. (Heath, 1983, p. 103)

In Roadville, on the other hand,

[y]oung mothers themselves begin to use question-statements in their talk with their baby, usually within the first month for the first child and almost immediately with subsequent children. . . .
    Questions in which the questioner knows the answer, indeed often has a specific answer in mind, are frequent throughout the preschool years. . . . (Heath, 1983, pp. 129, 131)

In addition to mainstream and educational books, articles on diversity in the classroom abound in professional journals. You will find additional suggestions in Chapter 5, "Resources." Teachers who read books and articles about other cultures, particularly cultures represented in their classrooms, will be fascinated by the richness and diversity of the human race. And for CRI, Guthrie, Rueda, Gambrell, and Morrison (2009), in their review of research on connecting cultures to the classroom, remind us that "classrooms that provide a closer match to the conditions with which students are familiar and comfortable improve students' engagement and produce better achievement." (p. 208)

Assessing Reading Skills

In other books in this series, you will find many assessments and strategies for teaching the elements of reading as identified by the National Reading Panel (2000): phonemic awareness, phonics, fluency, vocabulary, and comprehension. Those strategies have been found effective through research and can be used or adapted as part of your instructional routine with culturally diverse students as well. In this book, we focus on two of the five areas, vocabulary and comprehension. That does not mean we consider the other three elements to be less important for culturally diverse learners; it means those two areas are often especially problematic for them. Some of the strategies that follow can be used to assess both vocabulary and comprehension. Many can be used as instructional activities as well.

Assessing Vocabulary/Word Recognition

There is a confluence of research showing that vocabulary is a strong predictor of comprehension and overall reading proficiency (Anderson & Freebody, 1981; Bromley, 2007; National Reading Panel, 2000; VanDeWeghe, 2007). Of course, that makes perfect sense to teachers. If children don't know the words, how can they understand the text? Or if they can read the words but don't know what key words mean, how can they comprehend the text? The vocabulary book in this series (Newton, Padak, & Rasinski, 2008) identifies the following critical indicators of vocabulary/word recognition:

- Decodes words already in meaning vocabulary,
- Learns new concepts (or labels for concepts),
- Uses new vocabulary orally and in writing,
- Applies strategies to learn new words (structure, semantics, metacognition), and
- Uses reference works and other resources to learn new words. (p. 51)

The following assessments can help you determine where your culturally diverse students stand in regard to these critical indicators.

Cloze Procedure

The cloze procedure is good for assessing both vocabulary and comprehension. It is called *cloze* because it is based on the psychological principle that the human brain seeks closure or completeness to incomplete illustrations or objects. In the cloze procedure, the reader attempts to impose closure by using context clues to fill in blanks in an incomplete text.

The following are steps for assessing a student with the cloze procedure:

1. Find a passage that is of suitable length for your learner's reading ability and age.

2. Delete words throughout the text and replace them with a blank line. Here is a guide for the number of words to delete: If the text is approximately 300 words, delete every fifth word. If the text is shorter, delete proportionately fewer words. Leave the first sentence and last sentence intact.

3. Have the student read the passage and use context clues to identify the deleted words.

The following cloze was taken from *Barack* (Winter, 2008), a story for children ages 4–7 about the rise of U.S. President Barack Obama:

> Looking back, it's hard to believe how far he has come, the man whose name the world now knows—Barack Obama. This is a journey _____(1) began in many places. ____(2) began in Kansas, home _____(3) Barack's mother. It began _____ (4) Africa, home of Barack's _____(5).
>
> [*Answers:* (1) that, (2) It, (3) of, (4) in, (5) father.]

For assessment purposes, record the words that you deleted from the passage in a checklist to keep track of student progress. The checklist below shows the list of words from the example from *Barack* above with a column where you can indicate whether or not the student identified the deleted word. The comments column could include your observations of the reading (e.g., whether the student identified all deletions on the first reading, whether the student needed help in identifying a particular deletion, or the strategy that the student used to identify the unknown word). Add columns for multiple readings if needed.

Deleted Word	Correct Identification of Deleted Word	Comments
that		
it		
of		
in		
father		

The cloze procedure has several variations. If your student needs more support, you can place possible answers next to each blank or list all the deleted words at the end of the passage. The activity is then called a *maze* or *multiple-choice cloze.*

> Sometimes it was a _____(1) journey. When Barack was _____(2) a toddler, his father _____(3) far away. Sometimes it _____ (4) an enchanted journey. When _____(5) was only six years _____(6), his mother brought him _____(7) Indonesia to live with _____(8) new husband.
> [*Choices:* just, moved, Barack, was, old, to, her, sad]
>
> [*Answers:* (1) sad, (2) just, (3) moved, (4) was, (5) Barack, (6) old, (7) to, (8) her.]

If you want to see how your students employ both context and letter information for word recognition, you can give the initial letter (or blend) for each missing word.

> On the other side o___(1) the world, there w_____(2) half brothers, half sisters, a_____(3), and uncles. They wore d_____(4) clothes. They spoke a d_____(5) language. And yet, they w_____(6) his family.
>
> [*Answers:* (1) of, (2) were, (3) aunts, (4) different, (5) different, (6) were.]

Key elements in succeeding with the cloze procedure include choosing texts that challenge but do not overwhelm, giving students time and assistance in predicting the missing words, and encouraging students to share strategies and clues in identifying the unknown words (Rasinski, Padak, & Fawcett, 2010).

Assessment of High-Frequency Words

You can assess a student's automatic word recognition using a standard sight word list such as the Dolch (1955) or Fry (1980) list. Provide the student with a copy of the list; use another copy to record his or her score. Only count as correct those words the student can read effortlessly. The results can be interpreted as follows:

90%	=	Independent Reading Level
70–80%	=	Instructional Reading Level
<50%	=	Frustration Level

Assessment of Basic Reading Vocabulary

27
....
CHAPTER 2
*Assessing Reading
Instruction for
Cultural
Responsiveness*

Another resource for vocabulary assessment is Rasinski and Padak's (2007) Informal Vocabulary Inventory, which focuses on words from primer to grade 8. The words in the inventory come from Harris and Jacobson's (1982) Basic Reading Vocabularies. Using the interpretation of results listed above for the assessment of high-frequency words (i.e., 90% is the independent reading level, 70–80% is the instructional reading level, and below 50% is the frustration level), follow these steps:

1. Begin with the student's grade placement.
2. Read 10 of the 11 words to the student.
3. Ask the student to define or use each word in a sentence in a way that describes the word.
4. Give the student 10 points for each description if it is correct, 0 points if it is incorrect, or 5 points if you feel it is partially correct.

Informal Vocabulary Inventory

Primer	Grade 1	Grade 2	Grade 3	Grade 4
father	zoo	wink	wobble	tingle
hen	train	sharp	worst	vacuum
high	smell	possum	reward	sturdy
bird	quiet	perfect	stalk	yarn
people	money	overhead	presto	skull
thank	letter	breeze	manager	raw
youth	guess	hospital	lantern	pioneer
seed	draw	meadow	hoof	grocer
night	bone	apartment	ghastly	drought
open	beautiful	captain	eager	crimson
grow	always	coyote	cactus	confidence

(continued)

Informal Vocabulary Inventory (cont'd.)

Grade 5	Grade 6	Grade 7	Grade 8
rodent	visor	tutor	scant
violent	vague	tardy	phony
plumber	theft	sphere	rapport
labor	rotate	saliva	trivial
holly	rabies	pedestal	violation
revenge	plankton	peril	transmit
pursue	overcast	motto	foreground
fabric	habitat	jackhammer	merge
chat	fiend	khaki	joust
blurt	ecology	camouflage	doctrine
astronomer	employ	abacus	amputate

Source: T. V. Rasinski and N. Padak, *3-Minute Reading Assessments: Word Recognition, Fluency and Comprehension: Professional Study Guide* (2008). Reprinted by permission of Scholastic Teaching Resources.

Knowledge Rating Chart

A knowledge rating chart (Blachowicz & Fisher, 2009) can assist in monitoring vocabulary progress in a number of ways. It can be used as a self-assessment tool for word recognition in order to help motivate vocabulary learning (e.g., Faltis, 2005), while also monitoring word learning progress. The student identifies words from a text in three ways: (1) I know the word well, (2) I have seen or heard the word, or (3) I don't know the word at all. Once the student has experience with the word, then he or she can move the rating to the column that shows knowledge of the word.

Word	Know the word well	Have seen/heard the word	Don't know the word at all

A knowledge rating can also be used for screening purposes. For example, as a screening tool, you can identify words from the Dolch (1955) or Fry (1980) lists and record them in the Word column. Then you can use the other three columns to record the students' responses to your presentation and follow-up questions about the word. Another idea for the Word column is to use it for bold-faced vocabulary words that are found in specific chapters of texts in the content areas.

Knowledge ratings can be especially useful for comparing the words used by students of diverse backgrounds and words in books or their home languages. Recall that understanding students' cultures is the first step in being culturally responsive. Their cultures include the language they use. For example, for ELLs, listen to the words they use in their everyday language and add selected words to the Word column. Add a column to make the connection between the words they are using in English and the like words in their native language. This additional column can also be used for making connections between words in books and home languages.

Knowledge rating can be extended to instructional activities that are used for assessment. Word sorts, often used in instruction of new vocabulary concepts, can be created by using scissors to cut the words out from the Word column in the knowledge rating chart. Students can sort the words by concept (an open sort), or, if categories are added to the word sort, students can sort the words into the predetermined categories (closed sort). Words can also be grouped into the categories of the knowledge rating (i.e., know the word well, have seen or heard the word, don't know the word at all).

Assessing Comprehension

You may find that some of your diverse learners have adequate word recognition and vocabulary knowledge but struggle with comprehension. Teachers often say of these students, "They don't understand what they read." However, such a general statement doesn't capture the complexity of comprehension and, thus, doesn't provide specific information to help such students. The comprehension book in this series (Rasinski & Padak, 2008a) identifies the following critical aspects of comprehension assessment:

- Provides information on students' retelling and summarizing of information from the text,

30

....

CHAPTER 2

*Assessing Reading
Instruction for
Cultural
Responsiveness*

- Provides information on students' ability to go beyond the literal information in the text,

- Provides information on students' critical understanding of and judgments about the text, and

- Provides information about students' monitoring of their comprehension. (p. 61)

Retellings

One of the most common methods of assessing comprehension is through a retelling. As the name implies, in retelling the student is asked to retell what he or she read. Following are some guidelines for retelling (Rasinski & Padak, 2008a):

- Tell students before they read that you will be asking them to tell you what they recall from the text when they are finished.

- When students finish reading the passage, give them a few moments to collect their thoughts. Then remove the text from their view and ask them to tell you everything they can remember.

- Prompt students to tell you more when they stop. You might say, "Is there anything else you remember?" and then give them wait time. You can also ask them to give an opinion of the text or ask if the text made them think of anything in their own experience.

- Use the rubric shown in Figure 2.2 (Rasinski & Padak, 2008a) to evaluate students' retellings.

Two-Column Notes

Two-column notes are another way to gather information on the critical aspects of comprehension. Have students fold a paper in half lengthwise and label one column *What the text is about* and the other column *What the text makes me think about*. The first column will provide information on literal comprehension and summarizing. The second column can yield information about the student's background knowledge, whether he goes beyond literal information in the text, and whether he has critical understanding of and makes judgments about the text.

1	Gives minimal recall, if any, of a fact or two from the passage. Facts recalled may or may not be ones of great importance.
2	Recalls a number of unrelated facts of varied importance.
3	Recalls the main idea of the passage along with a few supporting details.
4	Recalls the main idea along with a fairly robust set of supporting details.
5	Provides a comprehensive summary of the passage, logically developed and with great detail that includes a statement of the main idea.
6	Provides a comprehensive summary and makes inferences that go beyond the text itself. The inference may be in the form of connections to the student's own life, reasonable judgments about the text or characters or items within the text, or logical predictions about events that go beyond the boundaries of the text itself.

Figure 2.2 Retelling Rubric

10 Quick Assessments

Here are 10 quick student activities you can use to assess comprehension. Some are suitable for narrative text, some for expository text, and some for both:

- Make a Venn diagram to compare and contrast the main character with yourself.
- Draw a picture of an important event in the story.
- Write three sentences that describe the beginning, middle, and end of the passage.
- Make a list of things you want to remember from the passage.
- Write two sentences: problem and solution.
- Do a story web.
- Write a letter to a character.
- Draw a picture of the setting.
- Write five questions you would like to ask the author.
- Write a different ending for the story.

These activities can be evaluated with a simple three-point scale: 3 (outstanding), 2 (satisfactory), and 1 (unsatisfactory). Chart the results and look for patterns across several of these samples.

Anecdotal Notes

You can assess comprehension very effectively and informally as you talk with students about what they are reading. Students can also respond to texts by drawing, acting, and making physical models or in other nonlinguistic ways. Use a variety of texts, including fiction and informational texts, poetry, and textbooks.

Most teachers ask students to make predictions during read-alouds or as students read silently to a designated point in the text. Such predictions are a good indicator of comprehension. Is the prediction logical? If so, the child likely has the background knowledge to understand and extend the story. Incidentally, when children make a prediction, avoid saying "Let's turn the page to see if Joey is right." Joey may have made a very logical prediction, but the author took the story in a different direction. Comments such as "Could that happen?" "Does that make sense?" and "Let's turn the page and see what the author decided to do" validate the child's comprehension.

Take anecdotal notes on the conversations you have with students about read-alouds, texts they read orally to you, and texts they read silently as well as notes on their nonlinguistic responses to text. If you write your notes on sticky notes, you can easily group them into the four critical aspects of comprehension and look for patterns of response for particular students.

3-Minute Reading Assessment

Another assessment option is the *3-Minute Reading Assessment* (Rasinski & Padak, 2004, 2005). This assessment samples a student's reading and determines his or her level of performance in four critical areas: word recognition, fluency, vocabulary, and comprehension. Basically, it provides the same information as most informal reading inventories do but literally takes only 3 minutes per student.

Assessing Your Instruction

Before adding new strategies and activities to your instructional repertoire, it is important to evaluate your current practices for CRI. What current instructional practices do you find to be effective? What instructional areas need to be fine-tuned? Are there instructional components that are not being covered to the degree that they need to be? Is there an area for which you need more information before you can self-assess?

To help you in evaluating your current instructional practices, we have provided a semantic feature analysis chart in Figure 2.3. Along the side of the chart is space for you to list instructional strategies you currently use to enhance children's literacy learning. Across the top of the chart are components that may be present in the activities you listed. Of course, not every component can, or should, be part of every activity. Some activities will encourage students to interact with classmates, for example; others may invite a more independent response. The key is to seek a balance in terms of the variety of strategies used so that a range of developmental levels and diverse learner needs can be effectively addressed.

Take time to complete the semantic feature analysis. Place a + sign in the corresponding box for each attribute that is present in a literacy instructional activity you currently use. More than one attribute may be present for each activity that you list. (It's OK to leave areas blank! We'll be revisiting this chart later.) You may wish to collaborate with colleagues; others may help you recall additional strategies that you use during the course of the school year.

When the semantic feature analysis is complete, it should help you see which aspects of culturally responsive reading instruction currently receive a great deal of attention in your classroom and which aspects may not currently receive enough emphasis. Knowing this will help you to better plan adjustments in your instructional routine. Discuss your findings and insights with colleagues.

Book Club

Instructional Strategies	Connection to Background Knowledge and Experiences	Students Participate Individually, in Pairs, and/or in Small Groups	Multimodal Response and Interaction with Text	Incorporates Multicultural Materials

Figure 2.3 Semantic Feature Analysis for Current Culturally Responsive Instructional Practices

Assessing Your Materials

A language-rich environment is especially important for culturally diverse learners. All children need to be read to daily, surrounded by print, and provided time to read independently; however, the need is so great for diverse learners that most will not be successful in school without these factors. Read-alouds, the classroom library, and wall displays should include multicultural materials because children learn better when provided materials where they "see" themselves (Bishop, 1992; Menchaca, 2000). When possible, materials should include texts in the native languages of ELLs in the class. Not surprisingly, the information conveyed in textbooks and lessons is culturally embedded. Some texts or topics can actually be culturally offensive (Meyer, 2000), so it is critical that teachers understand students' cultures in order to assess materials for such cultural disconnects.

The checklist in Figure 2.4 will help you assess the content of your materials for CRI. Place a check in the appropriate box, and make notations on specific materials.

Not only should you have materials that are multicultural in content, but also you should use multitextual materials—that is, materials that are different types of text and that represent different genres. There are four primary types of text: print text, audio text, video text, and interactive text (e.g., Kress, 2003; Lankshear & Knoble, 2003; Walsh, 2008). Print texts include books, magazines, and newspapers. Audio texts are those that children listen to, such as speeches and music, and visual texts can include videos, art, and other images. Interactive texts are those the child can touch or manipulate; they can be concrete or online. Digital texts can resemble print texts, as many e-books do, or interactive texts, if hyperlinks are embedded in the text. Here are some questions for your assessment of multitextual materials:

1. What print texts do I have in the classroom? What books? Newspapers? Magazines?

2. What audio texts do I have available to me? What speeches? Songs and accompanying lyrics? Poetry? Letters?

3. What visual texts do I use? Pictures? Art? Videos? Other images?

4. What interactive texts do I have? Online sites? Other texts that can be touched or manipulated?

Now that you have assessed the multicultural *content* of your materials and the *multitextuality* of your materials, what do you need to add to your classroom? Review the questions above, and make a list of what you might need to supplement your current holdings. As you assemble your classroom library, consider students' outside-of-school interests. Recall that one of the goals of CRI is to bring the outside in. In Chapter 5, we offer resources where you can find and evaluate print texts with multicultural content for adding to your classroom. You can also find resources for audio, visual, and interactive texts that will be primarily online. There are sites to find audiobooks,

	EXCELLENT	SATISFACTORY	UNACCEPTABLE
Overall Literary Quality • Authentic and robust language • Memorable characters • Compelling plot • Illustrations that support and enhance the text			
Cultural Characters • Presents common characteristics of a group • Recognizes individuality and/or subcultures within a group • Avoids racial or cultural stereotyping • Has characters that solve problems without patronage from a dominant culture			
Cultural Setting • Accurate depiction of time, place, or situation			
Cultural Authenticity • Portrays cultural norms and customs (i.e., dialects, food, clothing, religion, etc.) • Presents facts accurately • Has a main idea that enhances understanding of the culture			
Cultural Illustrations • Conveys cultural details • Is free of stereotyping or generalizations • Accurately portrays cultural settings			

Figure 2.4   Checklist for Content of Culturally Responsive Materials

speeches, and podcasts, for example, and sites where students can create and share content with peers for both comprehension and vocabulary building.

Assessing Your Instruction for Learning Modalities

Getting to know students' cultures, or background knowledge and experiences, allows for teaching to build on these interests so that students can be successful in school. But getting to know their *modalities* takes responding to student cultures one step further: It helps to build on their *strengths* and *needs* as learners.

Think of modality as the manner, or style, in which one learns. You may think of learning styles such as tactile, or learning through touch; auditory, or learning through hearing; and visual, or learning through seeing. These three modes (tactile, auditory, and visual) (Dunn, 1986) have been the basis for learning style research and are found in many theories of learning styles. One such theory is Gardner's (1983) original seven multiple intelligences: bodily kinesthetic, visual/spatial, musical, logical/mathematical, linguistic, interpersonal, and intrapersonal, as well as Gardner's (1999) addition of a naturalist intelligence, where the learning mode draws upon students' environment, or natural surroundings. Still other learning style theories consider whether learners prefer working in small groups or solitarily or prefer active engagement in or refection on the activities.

While there are a number of assessments that ascertain learning styles and modalities (e.g., Armstrong's Multiple Intelligence Inventory, 2009; Kolb's Learning Style Inventory, 1976;), it is less important to ascertain a student's particular learning style than it is to understand the multiple modalities of your students in order to create a flexible learning environment where they have opportunities to experience learning in ways that they learn outside of school.

Behavioral observation is one method that will help you understand your students' multiple modalities. Observe students during academic and nonacademic tasks and while they are alone or with others. Ask questions about what the child is doing while observing:

1. Is the child more often engaged in solo activities or peer activities?
2. What is the child doing while in solo or peer activities (e.g., drawing, reading, gazing, writing, talking, listening)?
3. What does the child do while reading (e.g., look at pictures or words more, use hands or fingers to point at words)?

Answering these questions will allow you to create a learning environment that leverages students' learning modalities in assessment; ultimately, the answers to the questions inform instruction. For example, if you find that one student tends to talk more when with peers, then a retelling assessment for comprehension might be a better assessment than a retelling using a graphic organizer that contains specific points in the story. For instruction, then, adding the visual modality of the graphic organizer during a retelling would address both the child's strengths and needs as a learner.

The semantic feature analysis in Figure 2.3 contains two columns that are specific to ascertaining multiple modes of learning. Now that you have thought more about multiple modalities, take a moment to review the strategies that you listed. Do students participate individually, in pairs, and/or in small groups? And with the strategies you listed, do students have opportunities for multimodal response and interaction with text? For example, when the learning outcome is to comprehend a fiction story in terms of the plot, characters, setting, or theme, do your students have opportunities to tell, act, sketch, use a graphic organizer, or respond with objects or manipulatives?

Assessing Your School's Readiness for Culturally Responsive Instruction

Tatum and Fisher (2008) remind us that nurturing successful readers "requires a wholesale transformation that involves a shift in teachers' beliefs and attitudes, and in schools' policies and practices, instead of simply tinkering with a few cultural additions to the curriculum or adopting a new teaching strategy" (p. 66). The following questions are adapted from DuFour, DuFour, Eaker, and Karhanek's (2004) work with professional learning communities. The answers to these questions have great implications for culturally responsive literacy instruction.

1. What happens in our school (or district) to facilitate the learning of culturally diverse students? Does it depend on the individual teacher, or do we have a coordinated plan?

2. What structures do we have in place that discourage culturally diverse students' learning (e.g., grading practices, teachers working in isolation, discipline, teaching strategies)?

Book Club

38
....

CHAPTER 2

*Assessing Reading
Instruction for
Cultural
Responsiveness*

3. Is our plan directive? Do we do "whatever it takes" to ensure that culturally diverse students learn regardless of home circumstances, parent involvement, lack of English proficiency, and so on?

4. If our diverse learners struggle with reading, is our response intervention or remediation? Do we address this struggle as soon as it begins, or do we allow it to build and then try to "fix" it?

Plans for Change

In this chapter, you have evaluated your own assessment strategies for CRI and, as a result, perhaps generated some ideas for change. Use the following goal planning chart to make notes about the changes you wish to make. As you do so, make sure that these changes reflect the "big ideas" we outlined at the beginning of the chapter:

- Focus on critical information.
- Look for patterns of behavior.
- Recognize developmental progressions and children's cultural or linguistic differences.
- Be parsimonious.
- Use instructional situations for assessment purposes.
- Include plans for (1) using assessment information to guide instruction and (2) sharing assessment information with students and their parents.

Also while goal planning, choose from the areas of culturally responsive assessment in this chapter:

- Assessing student cultures;
- Assessing reading skills: vocabulary and comprehension;
- Assessing your instruction: cultural connection, multicultural materials, multimodalities; and
- Assessing your school's readiness for culturally responsive instruction.

Now that you have identified the changes you wish to make, consider what you might focus on for improvement and how you will show the improvement with the following self-evaluation questions adapted from Hansen (1998):

1. What have I done well in my CRI this year?
2. What was the most recent thing I learned to do well in my CRI?
3. What would I like to do better in my CRI?
4. How might I go about this in my CRI?
5. What evidence might show the change/difference in my CRI?

You may want to share your self-evaluation with others to get their feedback.

Book Club

Goal Planning:
Culturally Responsive Reading Assessment

Goal _____

Plans by _____ Date _____

Action Steps: What do I need to do?	Materials/Resources	Evaluation: How will I assess the usefulness of this change?

Conclusion

Delpit (2002) reminds us, "If we are to invite children into the language of school, we must make school inviting to them" (p. 42). We can make school more inviting when we plan backward, assessing our students' cultures and learning needs so that we can then provide appropriate instruction. In the next chapter, we will offer some guiding principles for CRI and share specific strategies designed to help you teach "to and through their personal and cultural strengths, their intellectual capabilities, and their prior accomplishments" (Gay, 2000, p. 24).

Professional Development

ACED: Analysis, Clarification, Extension, Discussion

I. REFLECTION (10–15 minutes)

ANALYSIS

- What, for you, were the most interesting and/or important ideas in this chapter?

  _____

  _____

  _____

  _____

- What do you think will be your biggest challenges for assessing your culturally diverse learners?

  _____

  _____

  _____

  _____

CLARIFICATION

- Were any assessment strategies confusing to you?

  _____

  _____

  _____

  _____

- Which assessment strategies do you need to know more about?

  _____

  _____

  _____

  _____

EXTENSION

43

CHAPTER 2

*Assessing Reading
Instruction for
Cultural
Responsiveness*

- Share with your group other effective assessments you have used with ELLs.

  _____

  _____

  _____

  _____

- Which assessment strategies in this chapter will you try soon? Why?

  _____

  _____

  _____

  _____

- Are there any assessment strategies you would be reluctant to use? Why?

  _____

  _____

  _____

  _____

II. DISCUSSION (30 minutes)

- Form groups of 4–6 members.
- Appoint a *facilitator (timer)* and *recorder.*
- Share responses. Make sure that each person has shared his or her responses to each category (Analysis/Clarification/ Extension).
- Help each other with any areas of confusion.
- Answer and/or discuss questions raised by group members.
- On chart paper, the recorder should summarize the main discussion points and identify issues or questions the group would like to raise for general discussion.

44
....

CHAPTER 2

Assessing Reading
Instruction for
Cultural
Responsiveness

III. APPLICATION (10 minutes)

- Based on your reflection and discussion, use the following chart to develop a tentative plan for assessing your culturally diverse students.

Students	Information I Have	Information I Need	Assessments I Could Use
1. Name			
2. Name			
3. Name			

CHAPTER 3

Instructional Strategies for Culturally Responsive Teaching

46

CHAPTER 3
*Instructional
Strategies for
Culturally
Responsive
Teaching*

*A*fter years of teaching kindergarten and primary grades, Ms. McNair expects a wide range of literacy background knowledge and experiences among young students. Some of her students enter school from literacy-rich home environments where they've been immersed in language and books that mirror texts typically used in the classroom. They have an interest in books and even have favorite books or stories. They also understand what they read and extend their reading to multiple contexts. They will understand, for example, a linear story that begins with an event, continues with one plot, and ends with a resolution. They can connect the story with an event in their own lives.

Other children arrive in Ms. McNair's classroom from homes where reading storybooks has not been emphasized and their use of literacy is different from the uses of literacy in the classroom. They do not identify favorite books. They have fewer books per child in their public libraries. They may value nontraditional texts like music, video games, and how-to guides over more school-related forms of print. In addition, a growing number of kindergarten and primary-level children have native languages other than English. For all these reasons, Ms. McNair knows that she needs to recognize and identify the variety of background knowledge and experiences within diverse families in order to be culturally responsive in her plans for reading instruction. She wants her instruction to be supported by research. What research will Ms. McNair need to know?

Research on Effective Literacy Instruction for Diverse Students

If you walked into a classroom where culturally and linguistically diverse students were excelling as readers, what would you see? That is the question a number of researchers set out to answer (see, for example, Graves, Gersten, & Haagar, 2004; Pressley, Allington, Wharton-McDonald, Block, & Morrow, 2001; Taylor, Pearson, Clark, & Walpole, 2000). Here's what they found:

- Teachers emphasized explicit instruction in word identification, phonological awareness, and vocabulary instruction.
- Teachers maintained a balance between skills instruction and holistic instruction. In other words, not only did children learn word identification, phonological awareness, and vocabulary, but also they read complete texts and engaged in the writing process daily.

- Teachers assessed students early so they could plan instruction that would meet their needs.
- Teachers taught students to self-monitor their reading behaviors.
- Teachers had sophisticated knowledge of reading instruction.
- Teachers of English Language Learners (ELLs) provided structured opportunities for them to practice English.
- Teachers utilized students' prior knowledge to help them make reading connections.
- Teachers in all of these studies provided risk-free, highly engaging classroom environments.

47
CHAPTER 3
*Instructional
Strategies for
Culturally
Responsive
Teaching*

In addition to those excellent, research-based practices, we would add the following components of culturally responsive instruction (CRI):

- *Children need to make cultural connections with texts.* Connecting to background and experiences is essential for comprehension of new information (Pressley, 2000). Making cultural connections with texts is about bringing the outside—what students do in their homes and communities—into the text selection and instructional activities in the classroom. In Chapter 2, we suggested assessment methods for ascertaining students' background and experience, which include asking specific questions about what they do outside of school and observing their language and activities with peers. This assessment may be conducted through informal observations, in the form of questionnaires or surveys, or in the context of instruction as you ask children how a story relates to the people close to them. You can also learn about a child's home literacy when she brings in texts from home to share (e.g., instructions for a video game, letters from family members).

Literature can provide unmistakable contrasts in perspective and can help students understand cultural heritage—both their own and that of others within and outside of the classroom (Rasinski & Padak, 1990). Text sets offer one way to invite this sort of thinking. A text set is a set of books that focuses on one topic or area of interest and includes a variety of genre, such as fiction, informational texts, poetry, video, maps and charts, and so on. Perspective taking is another; imagine students studying the American Revolution from the perspectives of Anglo revolutionaries, Anglo loyalists, African Americans, Native Americans, the British, and the French, for example. Thoughtful, critical discussions that are touched with a sense of empathy can help children "come to realize their own cultural values

48

CHAPTER 3
*Instructional
Strategies for
Culturally
Responsive
Teaching*

and beliefs" as well as "appreciate the contributions of various cultural groups to our heritage and history" (Rasinski & Padak, 1990, p. 578).

Gay (2000) makes clear that CRI "builds bridges of meaningfulness between home and school experiences as well as between academic abstractions and lived socio-cultural realities" (p. 29). Au (2001) explains that diverse learners need immediate reasons for reading engagement, as opposed to long-term benefits of doing well in school. This is different from many of their mainstream peers, who tend to have the long-term benefit of school achievement modeled in their families. Instruction that focuses on the connection between student background and learning outcomes leads to growth in reading skills.

- *Children need to participate with texts in multiple ways.* They need to be active with their peers in both structured and unstructured environments. Participation is a focus of learning in CRI when the home culture is blended with the diverse worldview in which students in the new millennium are now engaged (Au, 2007). For example, children and adolescents are creating online content, playing video games with remote players, and accessing global culture through increased access to online resources and increased television use (e.g., Rideout, Foehr, & Roberts, 2010).

The classroom environment, then, needs to support maximum participation in literacy activities. Literacy centers, cooperative learning groups, and strategies that enhance peer interaction are some ways to increase participation. In Chapter 2, you were asked to identify strategies you use that involve participation in pairs and small groups; what you identified can inform your plans for enhancing student participation. Additionally, participation is one mode of learning among the student multimodalities (e.g., talking, listening, interacting) addressed in the next instructional principle.

- *Children need to respond to texts using multiple modalities.* A modality is a manner, or style, in which one learns and can be a tactile, auditory, visual, musical, interpersonal, linguistic, or nonlinguistic response. As described in the comprehension text in this book series (Rasinski & Padak, 2008a), nonlinguistic response requires the reader to dive deeper into meaning. Visual, gesture, sound, image, movement, music, culinary, and artifact collections are among nonlinguistic responses.

The assessment tools in Chapter 2 help ascertain the modalities that are strengths for your learners. The key, however, is not to teach to *one* modality. The perspective of multimodality in literacy "is the basic assumption that meanings are made (as well as distributed, interpreted, and remade) through many representational and communicational resources, of which language is but one" (Jewitt, 2008, p. 246). Clear in this statement is the holistic manner in which to view literacy and, as noted in this chapter, to make meaning with vocabulary, comprehension, and participatory strategies. Language-based modalities, including print, are only one of many, and the focus on multiple modalities connects to the real lives that diverse students experience outside of school and in the world (e.g., Gee, 2004; Portes & Salas, 2009; Reyes et al., 2009).

Multiple modalities incorporate both those that are strengths for students and those that students need to develop. For example, if you are using the read-aloud strategy discussed in this chapter for students to hear new vocabulary introduced in a particular book, students who have listening strengths could enhance their visual modality by drawing or printing words that stand out while you read. Students with visual strengths could create an alternate ending to the story or draw an image for a new vocabulary word and then share the ending with the class to enhance their speaking modality. The bottom line to responding to texts in multiple ways is the focus on using student learning strengths and building on their learning needs, which maximizes participation in the reading experience.

- *Children need multiple text types.* Text types include print, audio, visual, and interactive text (e.g., Kress, 2003; Lankshear & Knobel, 2003; Walsh, 2008). Print texts are those traditionally thought of as books with words in them. Be sure to incorporate a variety of genres when you use print texts, such as narrative books, magazines, information books, predictable books, poetry, and newspapers. Audio texts are those children listen to, such as speeches and music, and visual texts can include videos, art, and other images. Interactive texts, which the child can touch or manipulate, can be concrete or online. Recall the first CIU component in this section is that children need to make cultural connections with texts—that is, not only the content of the texts, but also the *types* of texts that students are reading in their home communities.

In their research on multiple forms of print texts in school and diverse home settings, Duke and Purcell-Gates (2003) found many print-based items that could be brought into the school. Home items included check stubs, mail, applications, fliers, bills, activity books, trading cards, coupons, lottery tickets, game-related print, comics, and comic books. These home items can be brought into the classroom in many ways. The Jackdaw strategy in this chapter is an example of using an interactive concrete text (object) to bring home and school together. Many strategies are also conducive to audio texts where students create music or speeches.

50

CHAPTER 3
*Instructional
Strategies for
Culturally
Responsive
Teaching*

Educational videos found on websites such as YouTube or TeacherTube (see Chapter 5 for video website resources) can also be used as text for vocabulary and comprehension. For example, Disney's *The Proud Family* cartoon episode "Culture Shock" (*The Proud Family*, 2003) has been the subject of many themed lesson planning sites and can be used with the vocabulary and comprehension strategies in this chapter. The full episode can be viewed online on free sites like Yodio (http://yodio.com) and YouTube (http://www.youtube.com), with a transcription of the episode on Livedash (http://www.livedash.com) to enhance the multitextual experience.

Having these principles and the research in mind, then, will allow teachers to choose or design exemplary reading instruction for diverse learners. The strategies in this chapter offer such instruction.

Guidelines for Instructional Planning

The remainder of this chapter describes ways to incorporate the principles of CRI to meet the needs of diverse students in your classroom. We begin by providing some guidelines for planning your CRI.

• *Create opportunities for choice.* Choice is motivating for students. For diverse students, motivation is linked to learner empowerment (e.g., Guthrie & Humenick, 2004; Guthrie, Rueda, Gambrell, & Morrison, 2009). That is, when a student has an individual goal that has an immediate value, the student is more likely to be engaged.

Note that choice is not about whether or not to do something. It is a choice between two competing options. A parent may say, "Would you like broccoli or beans?" rather than "Would you like a vegetable?" While you plan how to use the strategies in this chapter, think about choice. For instance, for the graphic organizer strategy there are different organizers that depict compare–contrast processes. A common organizer is a Venn diagram, which is two or more overlapping circles where the differences are listed on the outer areas and the similarities are listed in the overlapping inner areas. Circles are not the only way to compare and contrast; you can also present a graphic organizer with overlapping squares or with boxes labeled *similar* and *different* that may look more like a matrix or a table.

• *Maximize time for "eyes on print."* Becoming a reader depends in part on opportunities to read. Research from the last 20 years has consistently shown that students who read more at school and home achieve more in reading than do their peers who do not (e.g., National Assessment of Educational Progress 1992, 1994, 1998, 2000 [U.S. Department of Education, 2001]; Progress in International Reading Literacy Study 2001, 2006 [Martin, Mullis, & Kennedy, 2007]). Furthermore, noted ELL researcher Stephen Krashen (2004) maintains that free voluntary reading enhances language acquisition for ELLs.

To give your students opportunities to become readers, you can do two things. First, provide them with ample time to practice reading—to read!—each day. Second, provide access to authentic material that students find interesting and easy to read. Both these choices are associated with highly effective teachers (Allington, 2002).

51

CHAPTER 3
*Instructional
Strategies for
Culturally
Responsive
Teaching*

- *Be consistent over time.* A consistent instructional routine that includes authentic reading experiences as well as instructional activity in areas of difficulty makes lessons predictable for students and for you. This predictability leads to student independence, more efficient use of time, and greater on-task behavior. Consistent routines need not be boring. Vary instructional activities within the general framework of your reading curriculum. Who will read? How? How will students respond to what they have read? These questions and more can help you develop lively, interesting instruction that will foster students' growth as readers and offer them authentic, engaging reading experiences.

To develop this consistent routine, first think about the time available for reading and reading-related activities. Ideally, devote 2 hours each day to reading (Allington, 2002). Now break this large amount of time into chunks: How much time will you devote each day to read-aloud? To students' independent reading? Will you provide whole-group instruction? Small-group instruction? If the latter, what will the rest of the class do while you are working with a small group? To double check your decisions, think about your instructional goals: Are you providing students daily opportunities to achieve the goals?

- *Plan learning experiences.* In Chapter 2, we introduced the concept of backward design (Wiggins & McTighe, 2005). In this paradigm of instruction, the planning sequence takes the following order: (1) Identify desired results, which you will determine through pre-assessment; (2) determine acceptable evidence for success; and (3) plan learning experiences and instruction. The third step, planning experiences and instruction, incorporates the strategies and the instructional principles of CRI presented in the previous section. Therefore, consider the following lesson plan format as a structure to follow as you read the strategies in the chapter, so you can simultaneously plan how to bring it all together.

52

CHAPTER 3
*Instructional
Strategies for
Culturally
Responsive
Teaching*

First, in identifying desired results, decide what you would like your students to learn. What is the reading outcome? The outcome may be for students to understand vocabulary contextually (e.g., use knowledge of word order and in-sentence context clues to identify unknown words while reading) or conceptually (e.g., classify words into categories or understand new uses of words and phrases in texts). Or the outcome may be comprehension-based, like establishing a purpose for reading, comparing and contrasting information on a single topic across resources, or summarizing text by recalling main ideas and some supporting details.

Once you identify the desired results, determine how you will know that students have met the outcome. The vocabulary and comprehension assessments in Chapter 2 include authentic assessment methods such as interviewing and observing to determine what the student knows. For example, the cloze procedure in Chapter 2 is a method used to assess contextual vocabulary. Once you know your method of assessment, you must decide how to record whether the student has met the outcome. This can be done by using a checklist that states whether the student was successful or a rating scale, which in the cloze example could indicate how many words the student was able to complete. Rubrics are a third way of recording the assessment through determining what the student does to achieve the outcome in a quality way, what the student does that does not yet achieve the outcome, or what the student does to exceed the outcome.

The last step in backward design is planning the learning experiences. In a culturally responsive lesson plan, this is where learning activities are listed. The activities include the components of CRI threaded throughout this book: the strategy (specific vocabulary or comprehension strategy from this chapter), the multiple learning modalities (for response and for participation), the multiple texts, and the cultural connection. Use the following culturally responsive lesson plan process to address these elements, and, as you read through the chapter, return to the plan and adapt it as needed.

Culturally Responsive Lesson Plan Process

Step 1   *Learning Outcomes:* What are the desired results of the lesson? Consider your content standards, especially vocabulary and comprehension outcomes.

Step 2   *Assessment Plan:* What assessment method(s) will be used? Consider vocabulary and comprehension assessments from Chapter 2.

Step 3 *Learning Experiences Plan:*

53
CHAPTER 3
*Instructional
Strategies for
Culturally
Responsive
Teaching*

What strategy (vocabulary or comprehension) will help students meet the learning outcome?

What cultural information assists with the strategy? Consider assessment information from cultural interviews and observations from Chapter 2.

How are students participating? Consider assessment information from your assessment of instruction in Chapter 2 alongside cooperative, participatory strategies.

What multimodal response is incorporated? Consider assessment of student modalities through interviewing and observing from Chapter 2 alongside both strong and developing modalities.

What text types are used? Consider the four text types (print, audio, visual, and interactive), text forms used in the home, and texts with cultural content as ascertained from the instructional assessment in Chapter 2.

Instructional planning is your professional responsibility. As Pressley (2002) has noted, "There are no quick fixes with regard to improving children's literacy. There's no reform package that a school can buy that delivers improved achievement with certainty. The influences of packaged reforms are often uneven or small" (p. 180). Packaged reforms don't make the difference. Your careful planning and delivery of evidence-based strategies for CRI does.

Evidence-Based Strategies for Culturally Responsive Instruction

This section focuses on evidence-based strategies for CRI. As we explained in Chapter 2, this book focuses on vocabulary and comprehension strategies because those skills are particularly problematic for many culturally diverse students. We'll start with vocabulary strategies because research shows vocabulary is the best predictor of comprehension (Carver, 1992, Daneman, 1991; Stahl & Nagy, 2006). Although we have grouped the strategies, you will find that many of them serve to develop comprehension and vocabulary simultaneously.

In each of the vocabulary and comprehension subsections, we include ideas for utilizing multitextual materials and enhancing cultural responsiveness with further cultural connection, participation, and multimodality ideas. Although there are specific examples that

54

CHAPTER 3
*Instructional
Strategies for
Culturally
Responsive
Teaching*

accompany a particular strategy, many ideas can enhance any of the strategies in this chapter. Finally, the next section offers a closer look at structured participatory strategies to further support evidence-based, culturally responsive reading instruction.

Instructional Strategies for Vocabulary Development

The vocabulary book in this series (Newton, Padak, & Rasinski, 2008) divides instructional strategies according to three vocabulary development goals: (1) building conceptual knowledge, (2) using root word analysis and context, and (3) inviting word exploration and play. These goals are especially suitable for students from diverse backgrounds. The strategies in this section focus on these goals as well as on the instructional principles of cultural connection, participation, multimodal response, and multiple text types. For each strategy, we supply additional ways to enhance the instructional principles.

Vocabulary Self-Collection Strategy

Background

The Vocabulary Self-Collection Strategy (VSS) (Haggard, 1986) helps students of multiple backgrounds and abilities learn word meaning in context, while also using choice and peer interaction to build motivation and independence in reading. Ideal for connection to background, participation, and multimodal response, a pair or small team of students self-selects a word, decides why it is important to select, and then shares their work with the rest of the class.

Purpose

To build contextual word knowledge.

Multitextual Materials

A reading selection, either fiction or informational. Alternatives include signs, graffiti in the community, and instructions in a how-to manual with steps and associated images.

Procedures

1. Divide students into pairs or small teams.
2. Ask students to decide on one word from a narrative or content area text that they are studying. Help students make the decision by choosing a word that (a) they have never seen,

(b) they have seen but are unsure of its meaning, or (c) they feel enhances the meaning of the text.

3. Have students share with the class where they found the word, what they think the word means, and why the class should find the word important and/or learn it.

55

CHAPTER 3
*Instructional
Strategies for
Culturally
Responsive
Teaching*

Enhancing Cultural Responsiveness

Students can draw the word, select a predetermined set of words and create a new sentence, use words from multiple teams to create a story, or add self-selected words to a classroom blog with the word's meaning and why it is important. Additional participation can occur when the teacher models a self-selected word and invites clarifications as a class activity for the modeled word and for team-generated words.

Read-Aloud

Background

We are certain you know the importance of reading aloud to students. Did you know, however, that reading aloud to students can enhance vocabulary development even more than their own reading does (Beck & McKeown, 2007; Blachowicz & Fisher, 2009)? Read-alouds are especially important for ELLs so they can build their English listening vocabulary. It also helps them understand content, as ELLs' oral vocabulary is many times more extensive than their reading vocabulary. Research over the past 20 years (Schmitt, 2008) has highlighted the fact that hearing, saying, writing, and reading vocabulary words are multimodal ways for effectively engaging ELLs.

How much time do you spend in reading aloud to students? Your culturally and linguistically diverse students are likely already behind in their vocabulary acquisition, so double or even triple your read-alouds for them. Here are some procedures to increase vocabulary (and comprehension) though read-alouds.

Purpose

To encourage the child to participate through talk, to use vocabulary from the read-aloud in order to develop contextual and conceptual knowledge, and to engage in word play.

To use comprehension processes like prediction, reflection, and alternate story endings to support vocabulary learning.

56

CHAPTER 3
*Instructional
Strategies for
Culturally
Responsive
Teaching*

Multitextual Materials

A reading selection, either fiction or informational in a multitude of genres, including plays, poetry, song lyrics, and short stories. A read-aloud can also be delivered through a speech or audio-recorded text that is accompanied by visuals. Audio-recorded text can also be created for read-alouds by cutting and pasting online text into a text-to-speech Internet site, like iSpeech (http://www.ispeech.org).

Procedures

1. Begin by taking a "picture walk." Read the title and author of the book, look at each picture, and then ask students to tell you what the story might be about.

2. Don't change the words in the story to easier words. Students may not have heard a word before, but this will help their vocabulary to grow. Ask students what they think the word means.

3. At the end of the reading, ask children if there are any words they thought were interesting and could be added to a chart so that they could be used again and again in classroom conversations.

4. At key points in the story, ask students to guess what might happen next. A good guess is great even if the author chose to do something different. Rather than saying "Let's turn the page and see if you're right," say, "That's a good prediction! Let's turn the page and see what the author decided."

5. After reading, ask key questions such as these: What part did you like best? How are you like or different from [main character]? If you could end the story differently, how would it end? If you could ask the author a question about this story, what would you ask?

Enhancing Cultural Responsiveness

These procedures provide excellent springboards for multimodal responses for vocabulary learning. For example:

- Vocabulary from the text can be gathered to create new sentences or to develop an alternative ending that uses these or synonymous words.

- While listening to the story, children can create a character map. Vocabulary from story dialogue can branch off from the character's mouth (what the character says) or from the character's ears (what the character hears).

- Have students use a plot map to draw new images for a specific vocabulary word for the beginning of the story, rising action, story climax, falling action, and ending.
- Enhance participation through teams. For example, with the character maps, one peer listens for words the character says and the other for what the character hears; or each student chooses a different character.

57

CHAPTER 3
Instructional
Strategies for
Culturally
Responsive
Teaching

I Have, Who Has?

Background

I Have, Who Has? (Callella, 2006) was originally developed as a math game. In math, once students develop conceptual understanding of basic facts, then pairs and teams can match cards as a game. The game's success prompted teachers to use it in other subjects like science and language arts. It can be a great game for building vocabulary for diverse students because it incorporates participatory and multimodal elements.

Purpose

To enhance conceptual understanding of vocabulary.

Multitextual Materials

Concepts from content-area reading lessons or informational print, audio, visual, or interactive texts. Short informational videos on specific topics such as those from Ignite Learning's YouTube channel or its "free stuff" video page located at http://www.ignitelearning.com/res_freestuff.shtml (e.g., the 3-minute video *What Causes Earth's Seasons*, 2006).

Procedures

1. Create cards (as many or as few—as hard or as easy—as is appropriate for your students) with the vocabulary words you want students to know. Each card will have a clue that leads to the next word. The game will progress full circle from the first card to the last.
2. Randomly distribute one card to each student.
3. A student begins by reading the prompt on her card.
4. The person who has the answer responds by reading aloud his entire card.
5. Play continues until it comes full circle to the first person.

58

CHAPTER 3
*Instructional
Strategies for
Culturally
Responsive
Teaching*

For example, vocabulary for a text on the solar system might include these cards.

I have Earth. Who has Earth's only natural satellite?	I have the moon. Who has the tendency of objects to move together?	I have gravity. Who has another word for sun?
I have solar. Who has a word that means the path an object makes around another object?	I have orbit. Who has the movement of an object in a circular motion?	I have rotation. Who has the thrid planet from the sun?

Enhancing Cultural Responsiveness

I Have, Who Has is ideal for ELLs as they are learning English terms. For example, a card might say in Spanish, "Tengo *five*. ¿Quién tiene la palabra de Inglés para seis? [I have five. Who has the English word for *seis* (six)?]" The connection between first language and English terms in learning vocabulary has been found to be a predictor for reading comprehension (Lervag & Aukrust, 2010).

Language Experience Approach (LEA)

Background

The LEA uses a student's own language to develop text (Dorr, 2006; Stauffer, 1980; Van Allen, 1982). The activity can be conducted with a group or with an individual student. When used with a group, it typically begins with a shared experience such as a field trip or other special school event. The LEA for an individual student can be based on a personal experience, a family story, or any topic of the student's choice. The teacher and student(s) discuss the activity or topic, and then the student(s) dictates a story about the experience, which the teacher scribes word for word on chart paper. The teacher reads the story to the student(s), and they read it back. Such stories typically contain many sight words, and, as the students read the story back, they build their reading vocabulary.

Purpose

To develop vocabulary knowledge using students' own language.

Multitextual Materials

59

CHAPTER 3
*Instructional
Strategies for
Culturally
Responsive
Teaching*

Student's own oral language and materials with which to record that language (e.g., chart paper, overhead projector, chalkboard, computer for typing and printing, hand-held audio recorder, or computer audio-recorder software).

Procedures

1. Decide what story you will ask the children to share. A field trip? A community experience? A family story?

2. Decide whether the language experience will be from individual students, small groups, or the whole class.

3. Have students recall their background knowledge, either in pictures or in writing, before beginning the story.

4. Discuss their drawings or writing. Help them put these into a story structure—for example, a beginning, a rising action, a climax, a falling action, and a resolution. Or help them pick out three or four main points that they will include in the story.

5. Decide who will dictate the story. If in teams, will one student dictate, or will they take turns? If working as a class, which students will dictate and why?

6. Write the students' dictation on chart paper, or type it into a computer that projects the writing onto a screen.

7. Organize or reorganize the story as needed.

8. Have students choose words they know, know somewhat, or do not know from the story. Ask them to choose a number of words, which can be written on note cards and classified in a number of ways (e.g., similar meanings, knowledge of the word, similar onsets or rimes, parts of speech).

Enhancing Cultural Responsiveness

Some students may be able to type as their peers talk. Technological advances that allow for speech-to-text authoring include *Quick Voice Pro* for the iPhone, which converts 30 seconds of voice into text, and software like *Dragon Naturally Speaking* and *MacSpeech Dictate*. Regardless of the method, students can engage in a multitude of vocabulary and word recognition activities that are peer-based and tactile, including selecting words from the writing for word sorts.

Most importantly, students are using their home language and connecting it with standard English. For example, in *From Phonics to Fluency*, Rasinski and Padak (2008b) share the story of ELL Maria as

60

CHAPTER 3
*Instructional
Strategies for
Culturally
Responsive
Teaching*

she was involved in an LEA with her teacher. As Maria dictated, she alternated between Spanish and English (code-mixing).

> Autumn, Maria's teacher, uses these dictations to support Maria's English learning. "I'll add the English word using a different color marker to Maria's texts. That way when she practices the texts, she has the support of her familiar Spanish." Mrs. Gomez, a parent volunteer in Autumn's classroom, speaks Spanish. Autumn has taught her how to serve as a scribe, and she routinely takes Maria's dictation in Spanish. Then she and Maria translate them into English. All the children in the class have access to Spanish and English versions of the same text. (p. 159)

Sing and Read

Background

Research has shown that reading the same passage over and over results in fewer errors in word recognition, an increase in reading speed, and improvement in oral reading expression (Samuels, 2002). Music is indeed the universal language as well as a learning modality strength shared by many children, so having students sing as they read is a motivating and effective way to teach sight words or vocabulary words. In Chapter 5, "Resources," you will find a list of Internet sites where you can download lyrics of children's songs, including folk songs, songs about America, Disney songs, and seasonal songs.

Purpose

1. To invite word exploration and play with words in context.
2. To develop word recognition and automaticity.

Multitextual Materials

Lyrics and audio from students' favorite songs and songs of interest. Predictable books with repetitive phrases (e.g., *Is Your Mama a Llama?* by Deborah Guarino, 1989) or rhymes (e.g., *This Old House* by Karen Ackerman, 1992) are also effective resources to use with Sing and Read.

Procedures

1. Through conducting the cultural interview or through asking informal questions in or out of class, find out what your students' favorite children's songs are. Also play some you know in class to see which ones may interest them.

61

CHAPTER 3
*Instructional
Strategies for
Culturally
Responsive
Teaching*

2. The lyrics to your students' favorite songs can easily be found online when you type into a search engine the song name, artist (if you know it), and "lyrics." Post the lyrics of your students' favorite songs on large chart paper, an overhead projector, or an LCD projector hooked to the computer, and give each student a copy of the lyrics.

3. Lead your class in singing the song as you play it. Discuss the vocabulary and sight words found in the song.

Enhancing Cultural Responsiveness

Participation beyond singing and multimodal responses to the audio (sound) and print (lyrics) can include a number of activities. In pairs or groups of threes, have your students select a predetermined number of words that they know, know somewhat, or want to know. Or have them select words that have onsets, rimes, or roots that they are learning in class. They can create note cards for word sorts and put them into categories. Students can also use this multimodal text for the other vocabulary strategies in this section, such as VSS.

You may find the songs that your students choose are in the popular music genre. A number of online sources have matched popular music to engaging curricular materials. Flocabulary: Hip-Hop in the Classroom (http://www.flocabulary.com), for example, produces free educational hip hop music to teach vocabulary, reading, writing, social studies, math, and science in grades 3–12. Similarly, The Week in Rap (2008–2010, available at http://theweekinrap.com) offers "a week's worth of news, rapped" every Friday.

Word Banks

Background

Linguistically and culturally diverse students who need to build vocabulary will benefit from having personal word banks. A word bank is a storage place where students keep words that they have learned or need to learn written on note cards so they can refer to them as needed. Word banks are especially good for content area vocabulary.

Purpose

Hall (cited in Rasinski & Padak, 2008b, p. 124) notes several major functions for word banks:

To serve as a record of individual students' reading vocabularies,

To serve as a reference for writing and spelling,

62

CHAPTER 3
*Instructional
Strategies for
Culturally
Responsive
Teaching*

To serve as examples and context for group language study or
skills instruction, and

To provide reinforcement through repeated exposure to words.

Multitextual Materials

A reading selection, either fiction or informational. Alternative texts
include signs or graffiti in the community, poetry, magazines, audio
or visual texts, and instructions in a how-to manual with steps and
associated images.

Procedures

1. Instruct students that they will have their own personal word
   bank for a specified number of weeks. Let students know
   what will happen at the word bank stopping point—for
   example, reviewing the list, transferring cards to a different
   bank, or participating in peer activities like swapping out
   known cards. Eventually, some known words may be re-
   moved so that the word bank does not become too cumber-
   some to use and store.

2. Ask students to choose where they will store their word bank list:
   a notebook, computer file, page in a journal, folder, or page on
   the wall. Some teachers give students a large hinged ring, which
   they can open to add hole-punched word cards. Some teachers
   have students write the words in a notebook or folder. A recipe
   box allows students to file the word cards alphabetically.

3. Give students a specified number of cards for their word bank.
   Let them know that each time they know a word (as measured by
   using it in a sentence correctly, providing their own definition, or
   giving an example), they can add it to their word bank list.

4. Add to the word banks during lessons, specifying the types of
   words to add based on the objective of the vocabulary lesson
   or student knowledge of the words (i.e., words students have
   never heard or have heard but don't know what they mean).

Enhancing Cultural Responsiveness

The words can come from a variety of sources, and children usually
choose which words they will add. Cultural connections can be
essential with word banks, where text from home and community
can be a motivator to bring in words for the word banks. For example, ask students to bring in three unknown words from street signs,
television shows, songs, or home or peer conversations.

63

CHAPTER 3
*Instructional
Strategies for
Culturally
Responsive
Teaching*

Helman and Burns (2008) recommend that students just beginning to learn English focus on three new words at a time; students at intermediate levels can work on five new words. Students who are orally proficient can usually handle several new words simultaneously. Gersten and Baker (2000) agree that students should work over a relatively long period of time with a limited number of words.

There are many ways to add participation and multimodal response to word banks. Peer activities can include matching cards for similar sounds or meanings. Or, once a team masters a certain number of cards, team members can combine the cards to create sentences or short stories, sometimes with the help of sight words that might not be in their word banks.

Instructional Strategies for Comprehension

Although making meaning is important for all students, it is especially important for culturally and linguistically diverse students. Connecting to background is essential when comprehending new information (Pressley, 2000). This can come in the form of asking children how a story relates to the people close to them, choosing texts that relate to their community experiences, or having them bring in text that they have at home (e.g., instructions for a video game). Gay (2000) makes it clear that culturally responsive instruction "builds bridges of meaningfulness between home and school experiences as well as between academic abstractions and lived sociocultural realities" (p. 29). Instruction that focuses on the connection between student background and learning outcomes leads to growth in reading skills. Below you will find selected strategies that can work with different kinds of texts to help students make those connections.

Jackdaws

Background

The Jackdaw strategy, so named for a bird that is especially adept at gathering items to build a sturdy nest, involves the collection of concrete items related to a particular learning activity. Garcia (2003) reminds us that teachers of linguistically and culturally diverse students should support classroom talk and read-alouds with visuals, props, and realia. Jackdaws enable teachers to use students' culture and language as a bridge to instruction, while students engage in multimodal response (e.g., tactile, visual, realistic) with the alternate text of interactive objects. (*Note:* The term *jackdaw*, when used

64
....

CHAPTER 3
*Instructional
Strategies for
Culturally
Responsive
Teaching*

for a collection of artifacts assembled for educational purposes, is copyrighted by Jackdaw Publications of Amawalk, New York.)

Purpose

To enable teachers to use students' home culture and language as a bridge to instruction, while engaging in comprehension processes.

Multitextual Materials

A reading selection, either fiction or informational. Alternative texts include poetry, magazines, audio or visual texts, and videos of content area topics or themes. Chapter 5 includes resources for audio, image, and visual texts on the web.

Procedures

1. Select a topic under study for which it would be useful for students to bring in artifacts from their home cultures.
2. Instruct students how to choose an artifact from home: Is it connected to a theme in a narrative text (e.g., every child is special in his or her family; courage helps others; feelings make human beings; giving is a virtue)? Or is it a connection that children make between a story and their lives? Or is it an object from home that connects with a topic in a content area text like the seasons, shapes, or measures?
3. Have students brainstorm the objects that they might bring in. What can they picture that they have at home? What clothes, songs, pictures, letters, instruments, recipes, or other household items could they bring? Let them know that this is their first step in thinking and that, when they go home, they might have other ideas. Also ask them how many items they think they might bring in: One or two? Two or three?
4. Decide what students will do once they bring in their artifacts. Will they do an activity individually, in pairs, or in small groups? For example, individually, they could write a sentence for each object, share their sentences with their peers or team members, create questions about others' artifacts, or display artifacts on a theme. They could also use their objects to create alternate endings for stories or combine their objects to represent a historical timeline.

Enhancing Cultural Responsiveness

Cultural connection is central to this strategy, but so are multimodal response and participation. You can adapt the strategy by having students plan in teams what they might gather, decide on themes for the book, or select from a list of texts that have been read in class. A digital camera would be useful for taking pictures of artifacts for a class website or for creating a classroom blog on a theme. An example of a popular blog site used by teachers and students in K–12 is edublogs, available at http://www.edublogs.org.

Graphic Organizers

Background

Graphic organizers create visual representations of text structures. Narrative and informational texts may have different underlying organizational structures. There are myriad graphic organizers that help students make connections between a topic and their prior knowledge or cultural background and that help students make sense of texts. One example is the Herringbone. In Figure 3.1,

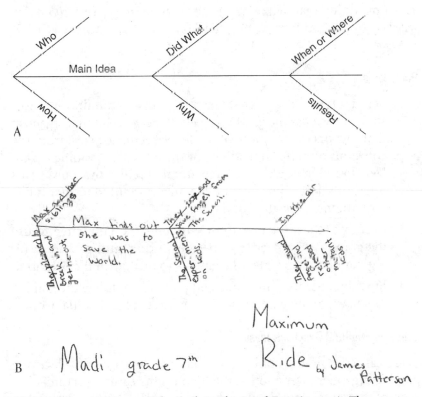

Figure 3.1 *Maximum Ride: Book 1. The Angel Experiment.* A. The Herringbone Graphic Organizer. B. The Sample completed by a Student for *The Angel Experiment*

66
....

CHAPTER 3
*Instructional
Strategies for
Culturally
Responsive
Teaching*

student Madi used the Herringbone (shown first) and answered each of the prompts (the main idea, who, did what, when or where, how, why, and results) for *Maximum Ride: Book 1. The Angel Experiment* (Patterson, 2007). In Chapter 5, "Resources," you will find websites with graphic organizer ideas and templates. In Appendix D, you will find some templates you can copy and use.

Purpose

To enhance comprehension processes using visual structures.

Multitextual Materials

A reading selection, either fiction or informational. Audio and visual texts are good first steps, as students can listen and interact with the graphic organizer. Predictable texts might also be particularly suited for graphic organizer practice. Types of predictable texts include chain or circular stories (e.g., *If You Give a Mouse a Cookie* by Laura Numeroff, 1985), question-and-answer formats (e.g., *Is It Time?* by Marilyn Janovitz, 1996), cumulative stories (e.g., *It's a Perfect Day* by Abigail Pizer, 1992), and familiar sequences (e.g. *Today Is Monday* by Eric Carle, 1997).

Procedures

1. Select a text. Decide what text structures it contains and how students will use the graphic organizer. Select a graphic organizer that mirrors one or more of the text structures. Select from the common ones in Appendix D or from the free graphic organizers found in books or on websites that reflect these text structures, or select story structure organizers to fill in elements like plot, theme, characters, and events.

2. Introduce the structures to the students, explain when to use the graphic organizer (e.g., before, during, and/or after reading), and give examples of elements to include in the organizer.

3. Provide students with a time and place to complete the graphic organizer, along with instruction for peer or individual work.

Enhancing Cultural Responsiveness

Peers can complete graphic organizers together or self-select one graphic organizer over another that depicts the same structure—say, a series-of-events chain that may be horizontal or vertical on a page. A graphic organizer can be combined with the LEA, where students can recite a story first and then use a series-of-events chain following the story dictation or they can start with the chain and then dictate the story. This is especially good for ELLs when combining English vocabulary with comprehension tools.

Multimodal response can include creating a comic or graphic story that shares the story structure. Students can use the structure for a new story on a new or related theme or topic. To begin, have students plan their story, and then divide the story into a specific number of frames that mirrors their structure. Students can use interactive websites to create their stories. Pixton (Goodinson, 2008–2010; http://pixton.com) is a website for educators and students that uses predrawn characters and layouts that can be manipulated by the creator, who also adds in the text. Creators can collaborate, and there are how-to videos as well as safety tips and tips for parents. ReadWriteThink has a character trading card creator (http://www.readwritethink.org/classroom-resources/student-interactives/character-trading-cards-30056.html) and a comic creator (http://www.readwritethink.org/classroom-resources/student-interactives/comic-creator-30021.html) where students can add text to existing story frameworks.

Concept Mapping

Background

Like graphic organizers, concept mapping is primarily a strategy that leverages the visual modality. With concept mapping, unlike graphic organizers, the student creates the structure—say, by starting with an idea in the center of the paper and then branching off into characteristics and then into possible subcharacteristics. This is different from having a preexisting graphic like a Venn diagram where the student fills in the structure provided. Perhaps the most commonly used structure is the cluster web. Students make connections between things they already know about a topic to be studied or summarize what they have learned through research or classroom instruction. In Figure 3.2, a student demonstrated what he knew about the topic of extinct animals. As you can see, Elijah decided to focus his concept map on Tyrannosaurus Rex. His nodes addressed the food, species, life cycle, and fossils of "T-Rex." No two maps from Elijah's class would look the same because students create their own structures.

Purpose

To make connections among elements (including text, self, and world) by creating a visual web.

68

CHAPTER 3

*Instructional
Strategies for
Culturally
Responsive
Teaching*

Name __Elijah__ Date __May 29 2010__

Cluster/Word Web 1

Write your topic in the center circle and details in the smaller circles. Add circles as needed.

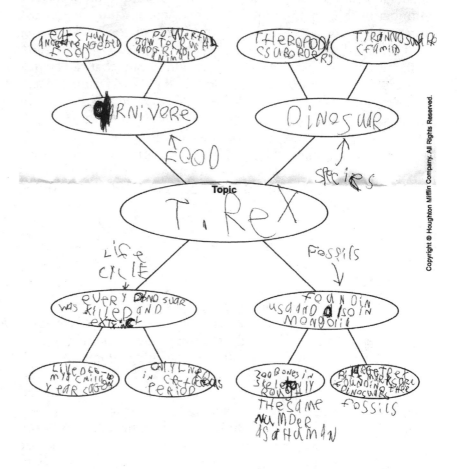

Figure 3.2   Elijah's Concept Map

Multitextual Materials

A reading selection, either fiction or informational. Audio and visual texts are good first steps, as students can listen and create their own webs based on particular concepts.

Procedures

69

CHAPTER 3
*Instructional
Strategies for
Culturally
Responsive
Teaching*

1. Choose a concept from a text or lesson that fits the student learning outcome (e.g., describe an extinct animal). Or ask students to choose from two concepts to begin with.

2. Write the concept in the middle of a sheet of paper.

3. Ask students to decide on which elements to connect to the concept. For example, the lines coming from the central element "T-Rex" in Elijah's map (Figure 3.2) are labeled with the elements food, species, life cycle, and fossils. Or have students draw a line from the concept to the first element that comes to mind. Some elements that come to mind with a concept map about themselves, for example, may be what they do outside, what they do on the computer, and what they do with their families or friends. ELLs can make connections with words or phrases in their first language. You could also establish a goal of a specified number of background knowledge connections or subconnections.

4. Decide what students will do when they complete their concept maps. Can a student combine his map with that of a peer who created one with a similar concept? If so, have the students make decisions about what from both of their maps would go well in a third map they create together. Students might also present their webs to each other and prepare questions about each other's maps.

Enhancing cultural responsiveness

Multimodal responses can include drawing pictures for the nodes in the webs, preparing questions to ask each other about their webs, and making their webs on the floor with cutout paper. Students could also role-play the nodes on the web, with each student selecting a node to act out or discuss while standing in the form of the web. Online concept-mapping resources for one or more pairs in the class take advantage of web interactivity. One example of concept-mapping software that can save, share, and print concept maps is *DrawAnywhere* (DrawAnywhere, 2009; available at http://www.drawanywhere.com).

Narrow Reading

Background

The Narrow Reading strategy (Krashen & Brown, 2007) is especially good for content area reading. Unlike the usual approach of including numerous books by different authors on a single topic or making

70
....

CHAPTER 3
*Instructional
Strategies for
Culturally
Responsive
Teaching*

many books on different topics available to students, in Narrow Reading students read texts by one author or about a single topic of interest. This approach enhances comprehension because the student becomes familiar with the author's style or with a single topic and therefore can concentrate on the content of the text. Narrow reading of narrative texts with the same author has been found especially to improve comprehension of and attitudes about English reading for students with limited English competence (Cho, Ahn, & Krashen, 2005).

Purpose

To enhance background knowledge and broaden students' reading interests as they become more proficient readers.

Multitextual Materials

Two or more reading selections, either fiction or informational, with the same author. Speeches from the same speaker, songs from the same artist, or a print text by an author and an audio book for a different text by the same author will also work well. Consider what texts students are reading outside of school in order to find multiple texts by a single author. For example, many video games have strategy manuals for different levels, worlds, or editions of the game. Or one company may have instructions for constructing a filing cabinet and constructing a desk or tips for mountain biking and tips for hiking, or there might be a particular blog or cyberzine that your students frequent. There are also graphic novels by the same author. One example is Telgemeier's graphic adaptation of Ann Martin's *Baby-Sitter's Club* series (e.g., *The Truth About Stacy*, Telgemeier, 2006a; *Kristy's Great Idea*, Telgemeier, 2006b).

Procedures

1. Choose an author who has multiple fiction or informational texts. If there is more than one author to choose from, encourage choice from students.
2. Select reading activities to accompany the reading outcome (i.e., vocabulary, comprehension, or a content area topic), whether shared readings, graphic organizers, or compare–contrast charts (Rasinski, Padak, & Fawcett, 2010) for the selections (e.g., covering story elements like characters, time period, and theme).
3. Decide how students will demonstrate what they have learned from the activities (e.g., make a presentation of their compare–contrast chart), depending on the outcomes and reading activities you selected.

71

CHAPTER 3
*Instructional
Strategies for
Culturally
Responsive
Teaching*

4. Have students prepare their demonstration of what they learned. For example, if a student will present a compare–contrast chart for comprehension comparing two or more texts by the same author, what will the student include in the chart? In the compare–contrast chart for four William Steig books in the comprehension text in this series (Rasinski & Padak, 2008a), the categories are

   a. Characters (animals or human?)

   b. Time period (duration of the story?)

   c. Does a transformation occur?

   d. Uses of alliteration? (p. 28)

Enhancing cultural responsiveness

The types of texts you choose are key for the cultural connections in Narrow Reading. Use peers or teams to explore what texts are used at home (as stated above, video game text, blogs, instructions, etc.) and how to select other texts by the same author. When home texts are brought into the classroom, you can incorporate multimodal responses that include artifact collections related to the texts or kinesthetic responses (e.g., the tableau strategy; see the comprehension text in this series, Rasinski & Padak, 2008a, p. 42) where students use their body or body movements to interpret the text.

Know–Want to Know–Learned

Background

Know–Want to Know–Learned (K–W–L) (Ogle, 1986) is a popular strategy, having been a subject of reading strategies research for 25 years. Although it is in the knowledge banks of many teachers and teachers may already use it in a variety of ways, it is important to revisit the strategy for diverse learners. The "K" in K–W–L is the priority question in CRI: "What do you *know?*" While asking about prior knowledge is best practice in cognitive models of literacy, it is especially important for diverse learners. We need to know their background knowledge and experiences. The focus on the cultural interview in Chapter 2 as the first line of assessment for diverse learners also reflects this priority. Students need cultural connections with texts, and instruction that brings in student cultures guides students toward reading achievement.

"What do you know?"—the first question—highlights background knowledge as an essential comprehension process. The second

72

CHAPTER 3
*Instructional
Strategies for
Culturally
Responsive
Teaching*

question—"What do you want to know?"—helps to arouse curiosity, while also teaching children how to formulate questions about a text. With K–W–L as a consistent, daily reading strategy, students learn to value questioning as a basic literacy vehicle. Finally, having students seek information and then report the "L," or what they learned, allows them to see the difference between what they knew to begin with and what knowledge they gained.

Purpose

To improve reading comprehension through background knowledge, questioning, and reflection.

Multitextual Materials

Any reading selections that are fiction or informational in print, audio, visual, or interactive form.

Procedures

1. Identify a topic in the text and ask students, "What do you know about this topic?" Encourage students to say anything they know or have heard about that topic related to themselves, other texts, the local community, or the world at large. Teachers sometimes ask what they should do if students share information that is inaccurate. Some teachers simply record everything the students share, with the intention of coming back to every statement as the learning proceeds. We fear, however, that by not addressing incorrect information up front, you may inadvertently send a message to students that the information is correct. We suggest you say something like "H-m-m-m-m-m. Let's put a star by this one. We'll come back to it later." In this way, you haven't exactly told the student she is wrong, but you have raised some doubt, and students will most likely pay special attention to that statement as they explore the topic.

2. Ask students to create two or three questions based on what they want to know about the topic. Show them different question stems like *who, what, when, where, why,* and *how.* Explain the difference between open-ended questions and close-ended questions, which have a yes or no answer.

3. Instruct students on the strategy or routine they will use to gather information that will answer their questions, the multitextual materials they will use (have them choose between materials if available), the timeline, and with whom they will be working.

4. Gather students together to share what they learned from their activity or investigation.

Enhancing cultural responsiveness

A three-column K–W–L chart typically accompanies this strategy, as Ogle (1986) introduced in her original description. This chart will enhance the multimodal response, and so will variations on the organizer and its use. For example, if a lesson has five topics and the class is divided into teams, one for each topic, they can collaborate with the goal of completing their accompanying chart. This participatory variation is also called Jigsaw (Aronson, 1978), as each group contributes their piece to the final jigsaw puzzle that the class assembles (see further explanation of the Jigsaw strategy in the "Participation Strategies" section that follows).

There are also many other alternatives to K–W–L in the research literature. For example, Huffman (1998) combined K–W–L with the "5 W" questions, also shown in the procedures above, and Mandeville (1994) added an affective column to the K–W–L chart, where students would add their personal value of what they learned. The personal value column connects to the idea that diverse students need to see how learning is immediately meaningful to them (Au, 2001).

Story Impression

Background

A Story Impression (McGinley & Denner, 1987) takes advantage of comprehension processes like predicting, questioning, clarifying, and summarizing. It consists of a series of words or short phrases taken directly from a story. The words form a list on the left side of a page, with arrows added between the words to depict the sequence. On the right side of the page, students to write what they think the story will be.

Purpose

To improve reading comprehension through predicting, questioning, clarifying, and summarizing.

Multitextual Materials

Any reading selections that are fiction or informational in print, audio, visual, or interactive form.

Procedures

1. Identify a text, and select words and phrases from the text. How many will depend on the skills of your students and the length of the story. The actual words you select may be sight words, vocabulary words, or words to aid in student prediction.

73

CHAPTER 3
*Instructional
Strategies for
Culturally
Responsive
Teaching*

74

CHAPTER 3
*Instructional
Strategies for
Culturally
Responsive
Teaching*

2. Write the words on chart paper or individual paper for peers or groups.

3. Instruct students to look at the words and individually or in teams construct a story that connects the words.

4. Have teams share their predictions; then ask questions about their predictions.

5. Read the story aloud, or have students read the story (or watch the video or listen to the audio you selected).

6. Ask students to revisit the story and clarify what the words mean within the context of the actual story.

7. Have students reflect on the activity by comparing and contrasting their prediction with the story.

Figure 3.3 shows the Story Impression created by student Jemu for the book *The Wolf's Chicken Stew* (Kasza, 1987). Using the words listed in the order they appear in the story on the left side of the page, Jemu wrote a short story on the right side, keeping the words in the same order. She also underlined the words in her story. Jemu then read the story and summarized it (Figure 3.4).

Enhancing cultural responsiveness

Story Impressions can link to multimodality in a number of ways. For example, a Story Impression, when combined with the language experience approach, could garner additional cultural connections. Students can create their own stories with language and then choose words from their stories for their peers to use to predict the story or create a new story. Story Impressions can also be a springboard to creating stories and sharing them online on a site like Mixbook (http://www.mixbook.com).

Participation Strategies

Recall that one of the four instructional principles discussed at the beginning of the chapter is that students need to participate with texts. That is, they need to be active within a community of learners (Au, 2007). The above vocabulary and comprehension strategies have elements of students working with peers and engaging in active participation throughout. However, many times it is challenging for teachers to focus on peer-to-peer interaction, especially with diverse students (e.g., Au, 2009/2010). Therefore, we have added this

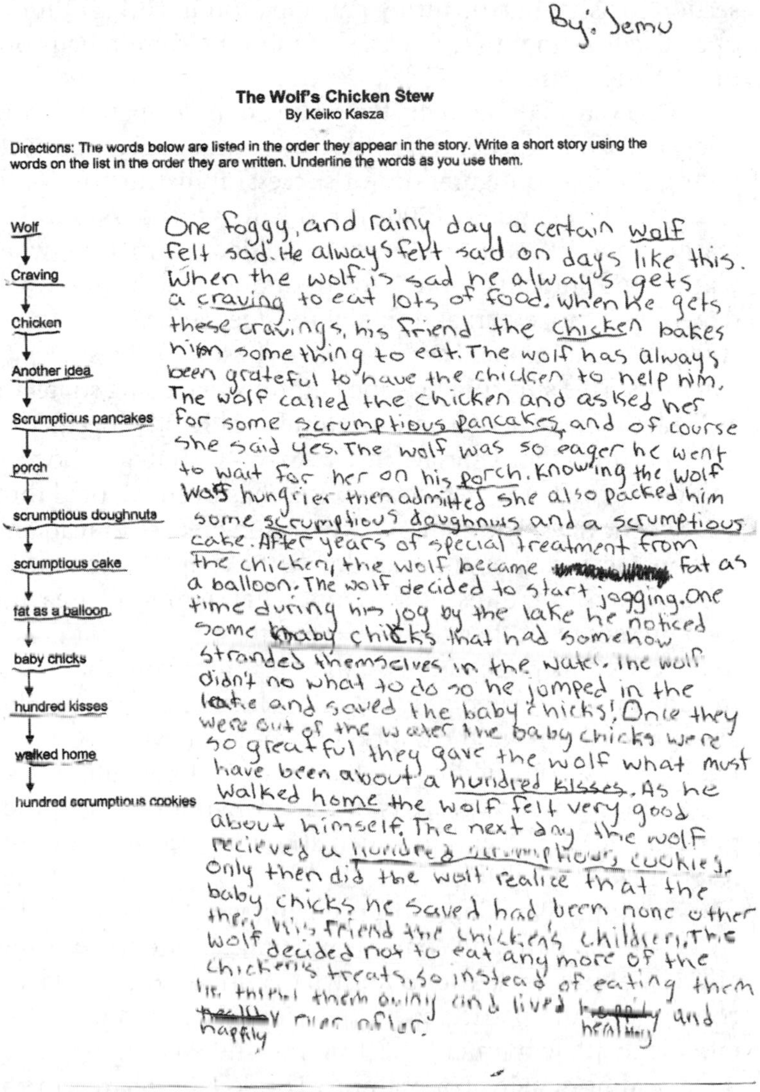

By: Jemu

75

CHAPTER 3
*Instructional
Strategies for
Culturally
Responsive
Teaching*

The Wolf's Chicken Stew
By Keiko Kasza

Directions: The words below are listed in the order they appear in the story. Write a short story using the words on the list in the order they are written. Underline the words as you use them.

Wolf

↓

Craving

↓

Chicken

↓

Another idea.

↓

Scrumptious pancakes

↓

porch

↓

scrumptious doughnuts

↓

scrumptious cake

↓

fat as a balloon.

↓

baby chicks

↓

hundred kisses

↓

walked home

↓

hundred scrumptious cookies

One foggy, and rainy day a certain <u>wolf</u> felt sad. He always felt sad on days like this. When the wolf is sad he always gets a <u>craving</u> to eat lots of food. When he gets these cravings, his friend the <u>chicken</u> bakes him something to eat. The wolf has always been grateful to have the chicken to help him. The wolf called the chicken and asked her for some <u>scrumptious pancakes</u>, and of course she said yes. The wolf was so eager he went to wait for her on his <u>porch</u>. Knowing the wolf was hungrier then admitted she also packed him some <u>scrumptious doughnuts</u> and a <u>scrumptious cake</u>. After years of special treatment from the chicken, the wolf became ~~scrumptious~~ fat as a balloon. The wolf decided to start jogging. One time during his jog by the lake he noticed some <u>baby chicks</u> that had somehow stranded themselves in the water. The wolf didn't no what to do so he jumped in the lake and saved the baby chicks! Once they were out of the water the baby chicks were so greatful they gave the wolf what must have been about a <u>hundred kisses</u>. As he <u>walked home</u> the wolf felt very good about himself. The next day the wolf recieved a <u>hundred scrumptious cookies</u>. Only then did the wolf realize that the baby chicks he saved had been none other then his friend the chicken's children. This wolf decided not to eat any more of the chicken's treats, so instead of eating them he threw them away and lived ~~healthy~~ and happily ever after. healthy!

Figure 3.3 Jemu's Story Impression for *The Wolf's Chicken Stew*

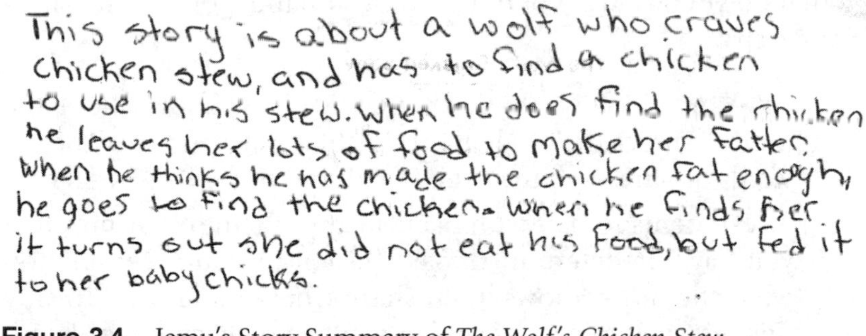

This story is about a wolf who craves chicken stew, and has to find a chicken to use in his stew. When he does find the chicken he leaves her lots of food to make her fatter. When he thinks he has made the chicken fat enough, he goes to find the chicken. When he finds her it turns out she did not eat his food, but fed it to her baby chicks.

Figure 3.4 Jemu's Story Summary of *The Wolf's Chicken Stew*

76

CHAPTER 3
*Instructional
Strategies for
Culturally
Responsive
Teaching*

section to assist in structuring participation in CRI (additional co-operative learning strategies are found in the comprehension book in this series, Rasinski & Padak, 2008a).

One way to think of the big picture of participation is a systematic move from teacher responsibility to student responsibility. In their grouping configuration for successful instruction for diverse students, Fisher and Fry (2008) start with a focus lesson where the teacher "does it" and then move to guided instruction, where the teacher and students "do it"; to collaborative learning, where students "do it" together; and finally to independent learning, where students "do it" alone. The "it" in these lessons is the strategy or lesson focus. This structure may be helpful when using strategies such as Jigsaw, Think–Pair–Share, and Numbered Heads Together.

We introduced Jigsaw in the K–W–L strategy above. It is a common group-oriented strategy that has been adapted for use in a variety of ways. For example, when students are to read an informational text chapter, they can divide the chapter into parts, which are assigned to groups of students. The members of each group then present what they learned about their portion of the chapter to the class. The presentation of their learning from the chapter can include the use of a graphic organizer like a timeline or Venn diagram, a word sort for the important words, or even a K–W–L chart. Jigsaw is best for dividing a whole into its parts and can also be used for longer-term projects or units where there is a product or performance at the end in which students engage in multimodal response to text.

In Think–Pair–Share, peers encourage student talk. The three steps—think, pair, and share—encourage students to think individually about background knowledge in order to make cultural connections and participate in the activity. Each step can be facilitated with a few moments of thinking and sharing before or during a reading activity. For example, Think–Pair–Share can enhance a strategy like K–W–L. When students are considering the question "What do you know?" about the topic at hand, you might follow these steps:

1. Say, "Individually, think about what you know about the topic." Direct the students to write a particular number of words or phrases in the "Know" column of the K–W–L chart.

2. Ask students to pair with peers next to them or partners that you have predetermined. Say, "Listen to your peer tell you what she or he knows; then share what you know." To vary this step, you might ask students to compare what they know.

How are the things they know similar? How are they different? You might also ask pairs to agree on knowledge that is unique or that has a particular personal or text connection.

3. Ask students to share their knowledge with the group. Students could share their own or their peer's knowledge, either by volunteering or by taking turns. You or a helper could record what students share so that all students involved can see the individual and shared knowledge generated. You could also invite other members of the class to comment on this knowledge by summarizing, extending, or creating themes.

Notice that the quality of the background knowledge is enhanced, since individual, peer, and group language produces more thought—and therefore more cultural connections.

Still in K–W–L, Think–Pair–Share can be used to generate good questions for the topic at hand. Think–Pair–Share can also be used on its own, taking only a few moments to make good predictions about a text or even to clarify or summarize texts. Think–Pair–Share can then become a common strategy where students are routinely thinking, pairing with peers, and interacting with the whole group.

Numbered Heads Together (Kagan, 1994) is another participation strategy you can use to get diverse students actively involved in classroom discussions. The strategy is designed to assure that all students' voices are heard, first in small groups and then in the large group. As such, it prevents a common cycle of classroom talk that looks more like interrogation than discussion (as shown in Figure 3.5). Such a cycle can be intimidating for ELL students or students of diversity who lack the background knowledge to answer the teacher's questions correctly.

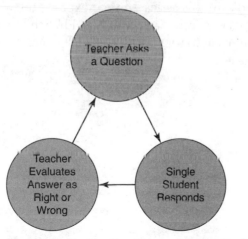

Figure 3.5 Discussion Cycle that Can Prevent Diverse Students from Active Discussion Engagement

78

CHAPTER 3
*Instructional
Strategies for
Culturally
Responsive
Teaching*

Numbered Heads Together is conducted as follows:

1. Put students into groups of four.
2. Each member of the group takes a number from 1 to 4.
3. Ask a question or pose a problem to solve.
4. The members of each group work together to answer the question. Stress that all voices need to be heard.
5. When students have had adequate time to discuss their answers, call a number from 1 to 4.
6. Students who have that number raise their hands.
7. Call on a student with that number to answer the question.
8. Call on students with that number from other groups to elaborate on the answer or tell how their group came up with the answer.

Obviously, the strategy works best with open-ended questions or problems that require discussion.

Conclusion

You've probably learned some new strategies in this chapter and revisited some you were already familiar with. Hopefully, looking at the "oldies but goodies" through a culturally responsive lens will take you and your diverse students in new directions. You will find additional vocabulary and comprehension strategies in the other books in this series. In the next chapter, we will look beyond strategies to specific areas such as English language learners, at-home literacy activities, students with special needs, and 21st century literacies.

Professional Development

ACED: Analysis, Clarification, Extension, Discussion

I. REFLECTION (10–15 minutes)

ANALYSIS

- What, for you, were the most interesting and/or important ideas in this chapter?

_____

_____

_____

_____

CLARIFICATION

- Choose one of the characteristics of classrooms where culturally diverse students excel and describe what it would look like in the classroom. What would the teacher be doing? What would the students be doing? What materials would be in use? What would the physical environment be like?

_____

_____

_____

_____

- Were any instructional strategies confusing to you?

_____

_____

_____

_____

EXTENSION

- Which strategies in this chapter have you used before? Tell your group how those strategies worked for you.

_____

_____

_____

_____

80
....

CHAPTER 3
*Instructional
Strategies for
Culturally
Responsive
Teaching*

• Which strategies are new to you?

_____

_____

_____

_____

• Think of a culturally diverse child in your classroom who is struggling with vocabulary. Describe that child to the group, and brainstorm ideas for helping that child.

_____

_____

_____

_____

• Think of a culturally diverse child in your classroom who is struggling with comprehension. Describe that child to the group, and brainstorm ideas for helping that child.

_____

_____

_____

_____

II. DISCUSSION (30 minutes)

• Form groups of 4–6 members.

• Appoint a *facilitator (timer)* and *recorder.*

• Share responses. Make sure that each person has shared his or her responses to each category (Analysis/Clarification/Extension).

• Help each other with any areas of confusion.

• Answer and/or discuss questions raised by group members.

• On chart paper, the recorder should summarize the main discussion points and identify issues or questions the group would like to raise for general discussion.

III. APPLICATION (10 minutes)

81

CHAPTER 3
*Instructional
Strategies for
Culturally
Responsive
Teaching*

Choose one vocabulary, one comprehension, and one participation strategy from the chapter that you have never used before. Develop a lesson plan for each.

_____

_____

_____

_____

CHAPTER 4

Beyond Strategies

*I*n the other books in this series, the "Beyond Strategies" chapter is set aside to address issues that do not fit tidily into other chapters but that are significant to the topic, nonetheless. In previous chapters, we looked at culturally mediated instruction—that is, instruction where teachers bring in the multiplicity of students' backgrounds, experiences, and communities and use that cultural knowledge in curriculum decision making. By now, you have thought deeply about your students' points of view through your assessment and instructional planning. We've used this broad lens to look at culturally responsive instruction (CRI), so for this chapter we decided to focus in on three specific CRI-related topics that teachers are likely to face in the second decade of the new millennium: (1) students with native languages other than English, (2) culturally diverse students with special needs and in special education, and (3) new literacies for the 21st century's diverse students.

To that end, we begin with sections on English Language Learners (ELLs) and the Latino/a population. (*Note:* The terms *Latino/a* and *Hispanic* are used interchangeably in this chapter.) The U.S. population projections show significant increases in foreign-born and Hispanic students in the next 40 years (see Chapter 1, Table 1.1), and these students need culturally responsive teachers who can understand that their native language is one of many facets of culture that they bring to the classroom.

Following the sections on these two language learner–based populations is a section on special needs and special education. ELLs and students from poverty have been found to be overrepresented in various disability categories (Blanchett, Klinger, & Harry, 2009; Xu & Drame, 2008). The Response to Intervention (RTI) approach to instruction can be used as a means to individualize targeted instruction for students from these populations and for others who struggle with reading and can now be used as part of the disability determination evaluation. (Also see the RTI book in this series: Wisniewski, Padak, & Rasinski, 2011.)

The call for "new literacies" for 21st century students ends this chapter. With technology central to the lives of children and young adults, including those from low-income backgrounds and other diverse populations, literacy no longer signifies only skill in reading print text. Like CRI, new literacies value the transportation of students' communities and world cultures into the curriculum.

Who Are They?

In 2005–2006, approximately 5,074,572 ELLs were enrolled in grades pre-K through 12 in U.S. schools, and that number is increasing. Figure 4.1, taken from the National Clearinghouse for English Language Acquisition (The Growing Numbers), shows just how dramatic that increase has been in recent years. Currently, among the states, California enrolls the largest number of public school ELL students (1,571,463), followed by Texas (640,749), Florida (253,165), New York (203,583), Illinois (204,803), and Arizona (152,962) (Short & Fitzsimmons, 2007). However, that distribution is changing as more ELLs enroll in suburban and rural schools in all parts of the United States. Further, school districts recently identified over 350 different first languages for their ELLs (Hopstock & Stephenson, 2003).

Year	Total PK-12 Enrollment	PK-12 Growth Since 1995–96	LEP Enrollment	LEP Growth Since 1995–96
1995–1996	47,582,665	0.00%	3,228,799	0.00%
1996–1997	46,714,980	−1.82%	3,452,073	6.92%
1997–1998	46,023,969	−3.28%	3,470,268	7.48%
1998–1999	46,153,266	−3.00%	3,540,673	9.66%
1999–2000	47,356,089	−0.48%	4,416,580	36.79%
2000–2001	47,665,483	0.17%	4,584,947	42.00%
2001–2002	48,296,777	1.50%	4,750,920	47.17%
2002–2003	49,478,583	3.98%	5,044,361	56.23%
2003–2004	49,618,529	4.28%	5,013,539	55.28%
2004–2005	48,982,898	2.94%	5,119,561	58.56%
2005–2006	49,324,849	3.66%	5,074,572	57.17%

Figure 4.1 The Growing Numbers of Limited English Proficient Students 1995/1996–2005/2006

Although we are speaking of ELLs as a group, there is indeed wide diversity within that group. ELLs bring to school a wide range of cultural backgrounds, literacy histories, and economic situations. Some families come to the United States seeking a better life for their children; some are forced to flee natural disasters; some come to escape violence in their home country. Many don't *come* at all— more ELLs in the United States are native born than are foreign born (Capps et al., 2005).

The Bad News, the Good News

The achievement gap is painfully real for ELLs. It is often difficult for them to pass standardized or placement tests due to language and cultural barriers despite the fact that they are usually allowed testing accommodations such as extra time or interpreters. For example, 75% of eighth-grade ELLs scored below the proficient level on the reading portion of the 2009 National Assessment for Educational Progress (NAEP), commonly referred to as the "Nation's Report Card" (U.S. Department of Education, 2009a). ELLs also drop out of high school at much higher rates than do native English speakers—31% compared with 10% (Short & Fitzsimmons, 2007).

However, "as ELLs enter our classrooms, they bring a wealth of literacy knowledge and understanding with them in many forms" (Warner & Moore, 2008, p. 14). The good news is that, with CRI, we can build on ELLs' solid base of lived experiences, family stories and celebrations, literacy histories, and cultural norms. By assessing ELLs' culture and reading skills and our own instruction and then designing CRI, we can begin to close the achievement gap.

What Do English Language Learners Need?

• *ELLs need to be encouraged to use their heritage language in the classroom as they move toward English literacy.*

Literacy instruction for ELLs has been steeped in controversy for decades. Should students be encouraged, or even allowed, to use their first language, or will they assimilate into the classroom more quickly if they are instructed in English only? CRI requires that we honor and utilize students' background knowledge and experiences. With all students, you begin with what they already know; the only difference with ELLs is that their heritage language is the vehicle by which to connect with their backgrounds. Numerous research studies show that literacy competence in the first language will transfer to English literacy (Greene, 1999; Krashen, 2004; Krashen & McField, 2005; Oller & Eilers, 2002; Willig, 1985).

Sometimes teachers worry that they cannot teach an ELL effectively because they don't know the student's heritage language. We asked some of the best ELL teachers we know for some insight into this concern. Lynne Smith has taught ELLs of "both sexes, young adults through grandmothers, and all nationalities." She reminded us of the primary task before us: "Your task is to make English structure as simple and clear as possible. Give students confidence in the *structure* of English rather than worry about translation."

Echevarria, Vogt, and Short (2010, p. 82) describe this clarity as comprehensible input and offer an example of what responses students might give at different levels of English proficiency in describing a story setting:

Beginning: "Cold day."

Early Intermediate: "The day is cold and there is snow."

Intermediate: "The day is very cold and heavy snow is falling."

Honey Massey, who has taught K–12 ELLs for 22 years, described the language skills of new ELLs in the classroom and went on to reinforce what we have said repeatedly in this book:

> ESL children and even adults must feel comfortable in order to venture into a new language and a new learning style. For the first part of their learning experience they will be hesitant to open their mouth to speak but they are absorbing a lot. This is like a baby who observes what is in his/her surroundings but does not have the ability to respond. Unfortunately the classroom teacher is facing 25 children who do know the language and can't slow down the entire class. They can provide all written material, they can use visuals, and ask another student to mentor the ESL student. Again, a simple gesture but so important is to show a genuine interest in the culture and lifestyle of the ESL child, perhaps sharing some information with the entire class if the ESL child is not able to articulate anything about his/her country of origin.

• *ELLs need time.* While conversational language is typically acquired in 1 to 2 years, it can take 6 to 9 years for ELLs to achieve proficiency in academic English. Unfortunately, conversational language is often mistaken for overall English proficiency, resulting in educational support services being discontinued for ELLs. Compounding this travesty, the transition away from support services may happen when ELLs are moving to grade levels that rely heavily on academic language for content area learning. Then these students often are mistaken for slower learners and placed in special education classes, are frequently retained, or end up dropping out of school (August & Hakuta, 1997).

As a classroom teacher, you are probably not directly responsible for the assignment of support services or special education placements. However, your input is critical when administrative decisions are made around these issues. Carefully document areas of interventions, successes, and learning needs of your ELLs. Be sure to include quantitative as well as qualitative data; anecdotes are not enough. Read up on the language development of ELLs, and share what you learn with your colleagues and administrators. The fact that ELLs are disproportionately placed in special education or retained in grade level most often stems from ignorance, not prejudice. Do all you can to help others become informed.

• *ELLs need appropriate reading materials.* They need to see themselves in classroom materials. Include in your classroom both literary and informational books, pictures, bulletin boards, and other resources from the ELLs' home cultures. The National Council of Teachers of English (2006) set forth the following guidelines for selecting materials for ELLs:

- Materials should include culturally relevant texts.
- Authentic materials should be written to inform or entertain, not to teach a grammar point or a letter–sound correspondence.
- The language of the text should be natural.
- If translated, the translation should be good language.
- Materials should include predictable text for emergent readers.
- Materials should include texts with nonlinguistic cues that support comprehension.

Instructional Strategies for English Language Learners

In Chapter 3, you read about Autumn, a teacher who utilized a student's heritage language as the student dictated a story during a language experience activity. As you will recall, Autumn used different-colored markers for the Spanish and English words her student used. As our ELL colleagues above reminded us, you don't have to be proficient in all your students' heritage languages as they move toward English literacy. Autumn enlisted the aid of a parent volunteer who spoke Spanish to provide extra support for Maria. You can also use older students or community volunteers who speak the same language. When using the Language Experience Approach, the text can be written in a student's home language and translated into English or vice versa. The child can take the story home to practice with her family, thus providing cultural affirmation simultaneously with English literacy for the entire family (Cummins et al., 2005). Many teachers report that using ELLs' language in the classroom also provides a benefit for English-speaking students who informally start picking up on the ELLs' language.

The National Council of Teachers of English (2006) suggests having ELLs read more accessible texts on a topic before reading the assigned text. Your school librarian or children's librarian at the public library can help you locate high-interest, low-readability materials on topics you will be studying. An engaging and productive strategy is to have your students create a classroom library of topics for your curriculum. After a unit of study, have students write and illustrate "skinny books" summarizing what they learned. The books can be kept from year to year so that you have a wide variety of information and illustrations on any one topic, and the materials will be more accessible for your ELLs because they are all written in kid-language. Of course, this strategy has benefits beyond providing accessible texts for your ELLs. Students who create the skinny books must review the material, learn the skill of summarizing, and practice their writing skills. The books are popular reading with non-ELL students as well as ELLs; students enjoy reading the books written by neighbors, friends, and siblings from previous years. You can also use the books as an assessment of what the students learned. ELL students may want to make bilingual dictionaries for their own use and then leave them in the classroom for future ELLs.

Below are a few more instructional suggestions from the National Council of Teachers of English (2006):

- Replace discrete skill exercises and drills with many opportunities to read.
- Provide opportunities for silent reading in either the students' first language or English.
- Read aloud frequently to allow students to become familiar with and appreciate the sounds and structures of written language.
- Read aloud while students have access to the text to facilitate connecting oral and written modalities.

- Stimulate students' content knowledge of the text before introducing the text.
- Teach language features, such as text structure, vocabulary, and text- and sentence-level grammar, to facilitate comprehension of the text.

Sharon Hamad, a teacher of elementary and secondary ELLs for 15 years, gave us a few practical tips:

- Upon receiving an ELL student, pair him with a native English classmate.
- Seat your ELL close to the front of the classroom.
- Take several trips around the school environment to familiarize the student with important areas such as the restrooms, cafeteria, and school office. Introduce him to the nurse, principal, secretary, and so on.
- When speaking directly to the student, eye-to-eye contact, tone of voice, and helpful gestures and visuals are important.
- Don't assume ELL students understand your words. They don't always understand what they don't understand. Ask them to repeat your directions or assignments, have them show you what they are to do, have them show you which book they are working from, and so on.
- Repetition is very important; students will not always "get it" the first time.
- Label the classroom: blackboard, clock, exit, window, and so on.

Although paper-and-pencil tests are frequently required for state and other standardized tests, you should embed evaluation in instructional activities as often as you can. Allow ELLs a variety of ways to show what they know nonverbally as well as verbally. You can use graphic organizers, role plays, art, journals, discussions, oral interviews, and other authentic assessments.

Latino/a Populations

Who Are They?

Native Spanish speakers make up 82% of ELLs in the United States, and the U.S. Census Bureau predicts that by 2021 one in four U.S. students will be Latino/a (Planty, Kena, & Hannes, 2009). While past history may cause us to mentally place Latino/a students in California, Florida, and Texas, currently the biggest increase in the Latino/a population is in the mid-Atlantic states (Rico, 2010). Latino/a children are more than twice as likely to be poor as white children are. At least one-third of Latino/a families lack health insurance (Berliner, 2009); consequently, Latino/a children often come to school with health problems that interfere with their learning. Keep in mind, however, that there is no one-size-fits-all Hispanic family. Each child comes with her own socioeconomic status, cultural characteristics, language proficiency, and literacy background.

The Bad News, the Good News

Sixteen percent of Hispanic students scored at or above proficient in reading on the 2009 National Assessment of Educational Progress, compared with 39% of white students (U.S. Department of Education, 2009a). Further, Hansen (2005) found Hispanic students are more likely than white students:

- To enter kindergarten underprepared for learning,
- To be retained in a grade,
- To be suspended or expelled,
- To drop out of school (twice the rate of whites), and
- To fail to enroll in and complete college. When they do enter college, Hispanic students are more likely than white students to pursue a two-year associate's degree than a bachelor's degree.

Adding to the problems of cultural and language barriers, Hispanics make up a large portion of migrant farm workers in the United States, which results in lack of continuity in their children's education because they frequently change schools.

As with all ELLs, however, the good news is these students come to school with rich schemas on which to build. Moll has studied learning among Hispanic children for decades. He challenges us to "think of literacy (or literacies) as particular ways of using language for a variety of purposes, as a socio-cultural practice with intellectual significance" (Moll, 1994, p. 201). By studying families in their own settings in the southwestern U.S., Moll has documented the extensive knowledge that exists in a typical Hispanic community—for example, knowledge about different soils, cultivation of plants, water distribution and management, animal husbandry, veterinary medicine, ranch economics, and mechanics as well as a host of other areas.

Wise teachers seek out these sociocultural literacies among their students. In doing so, they are able to help diverse students bridge the gap between their culture-specific schemas and traditional reading instruction. Most importantly, these teachers view literacy through a lens that transcends school-bound reading and writing and values the "curriculum from the world of the home" (Heath, 1983, p. 340).

The National Center for Education Statistics has, in conjunction with its Early Childhood Longitudinal Study, compiled a database of 19,590 kindergarteners that compares the social skills of children from different ethnic and racial groups when they begin school. The study has looked at several social areas, including self-control, interpersonal skills, approaches to learning, and internalizing and externalizing problem behaviors. Researchers have found that a majority of Latino/a children enter kindergarten with the same social skills as middle-class white children. Espinosa (quoted in Zehr, 2010) concluded, "We have some evidence of real capabilities [in Latino/a youngsters] that our school people are missing once academics start to take center stage."

What Do Latino/a Students Need?

Because Latino/a students make up such a large proportion of ELLs in our schools, what we have written in the section on the needs of ELLs applies. In addition to the suggestions above, it is important that teachers and schools look beyond the academic needs to advocate for social services such as health care, child care, and nutrition that a number of Latino families need.

Instructional Strategies for Latino/a Students

All of the instructional strategies listed above for ELLs are applicable for Hispanic students. Following are a few additional suggestions:

- Make reading groups and cooperative learning groups heterogeneous so that you eliminate the stigma of "low reader" and so that struggling Hispanic students can interact with more proficient classmates.
- Have older students write their own autobiographies to affirm their heritage, while providing writing practice.
- Refrain from making statements that might be embarrassing to Latino/a students. For example, don't ask what students are doing for the weekend; a Latino/a student may be helping his migrant family pick crops.

- Consider family contexts when assigning homework. For example, some students may have work at home that may not allow for homework time.
- Remember, Hispanic families vary greatly. Don't ask Hispanic students to speak for the entire group (e.g., How do Cubans feel about the United States?).

In the other books in this series, you will find suggestions for literacy instruction for ELLs and Hispanic students.

Diverse Students with Special Needs and Students in Special Education

Who Are They?

Students in special education constitute about 9% of the U.S. general population between the ages of 6 and 21 (U.S. Department of Education, 2009b). These students have a diagnosis under one or more of the 13 categories of disability in the Individuals with Disabilities Education Act (IDEA), which is the federal law first enacted in 1975 as the Education for All Handicapped Children Act.

Within the 13 diagnostic categories, the learning disability category has been a subject of great controversy because of both the high incidence of diagnoses and the overidentification of those in culturally diverse groups. Since 1975, the diagnoses have increased threefold; as a result, at least half of all children in special education are classified as having a learning disability. The continued rise in diagnosis could be averted, say researchers and policy makers, with targeted, research-based instructional approaches for students who struggle with reading (Fuchs & Fuchs, 2005). Response to Intervention (RTI) is such an approach.

RTI is a three-tiered model: The first tier is instruction for most students (about 80% in the classroom), the second tier is more targeted instruction for struggling students (about 10–15%), and the third tier is the most intensive and most frequent instruction for a few students (about 5%). The struggling students in Tier 2 are considered those with special needs; in reading, these children tend to have fewer reading skills than their peers do, gain new reading skills more slowly than their peers do, and/or have achievement scores in reading that are lower than their own ability suggests they should be (e.g., Vaughn & Fuchs, 2003). The goal of the targeted instruction in

Tier 2 is to narrow the reading gap between students with special needs and their Tier 1 peers. When students in Tier 2 do not respond to interventions according to progress monitoring, then they move to Tier 3 for the most intensive intervention; the evaluation of the response to Tier 2 intervention can be used as part of a disability determination (IDEA, 2004).

The Bad News, the Good News

We have already mentioned the high incidence of learning disability diagnoses among those in culturally diverse groups. For example, among students ages 6–12, Native American and black/not Hispanic students were 1.5 times more likely in 2003 to be receiving services in special education than was a combination of Asian/ Pacific Islanders, Hispanic students, and white/not Hispanic students (U.S. Department of Education, 2009b).

The dropout rates of students with disabilities are also a problem. In 2003, about 52% of students with disabilities age 14 or older graduated from high school, with 33.6% dropping out. Asian/Pacific Islander students and white students were most likely to graduate, and the least likely were black (U.S. Department of Education, 2009b). While dropout rates for students with disabilities are problematic, the good news for these students includes new efforts in dropout prevention like the National Dropout Prevention Center for Students with Disabilities (NDPC–SD), RTI, and inclusion service-delivery models.

Started in 2004, the NDPC–SD (http://www.ndpc-sd.org) is funded by the U.S. Department of Education and has the goal of assisting school districts in lowering dropout rates and increasing school completion rates for students with disabilities. It synthesizes research to help in implementing research-based practices and supports further research and practice with coaching and technical assistance. For example, the NDPC–SD provides information on evidence-based dropout prevention programs in New Hampshire and Iowa and on cognitive behavioral interventions that are linked to reading achievement.

RTI as an approach to instruction and evaluation can quell disability determinations for diverse populations that are overrepresented in special education. Additionally, collaborative structures connecting general and special education that support inclusion (e.g., co-teaching by general classroom teachers and intervention specialists) can help to prevent such inequity. Research on co-teaching shows higher achievement and improved social skills for students with disabilities and struggling students in diverse classrooms (Walther-Thomas, 1997). Additionally, peer tutoring and mixed ability grouping within the regular classroom have been shown to result in reading gains for elementary students with reading disabilities (e.g., Chard, Vaughn, & Tyler, 2002).

What Do Diverse Students with Special Needs and Students in Special Education Need?

They need research-based reading practices like the ones presented in this *Evidence-Based Reading Instruction* series. In fact, educators are required by IDEA and the No Child Left Behind Act of 2001 to use evidence-based practices (Council for Exceptional Children, 2006). Evidence-based instruction is also central to RTI. RTI is, "simply put, a process of implementing high-quality scientifically validated instructional practices based on learner needs, monitoring student progress, and adjusting instruction based on the student's response" (Bender & Shores, 2007, p. 7). Notice the similarity to CRI: Teachers *respond* to individual student needs and progress. Also, RTI instructional principles compare to those of CRI in other ways. For example, instruction for students with special needs should focus on both peer interaction and visual scaffolds (Wisniewski, Padak, & Rasinski, 2011). Peer interaction is one essential ingredient in CRI: Students must participate. Visual scaffolds are central to both multitextual materials and multimodal response for diverse students. Additionally, as with diverse students, students with disabilities benefit from connecting new information to existing background knowledge and experience (e.g., Deshler et al., 2001). Therefore, students benefit when teachers use both an RTI and a CRI lens.

Instructional Strategies for Diverse Students with Special Needs and Special Education

In the RTI book in this series (Wisniewski, Padak, & Rasinski, 2011), you will find suggestions for research-based literacy practices for students with special needs, many that are also beneficial for students with disabilities. The following is a process to follow from the RTI lens:

1. Identify students who need targeted assistance in the classroom.

2. Plan the assistance based on the learning outcomes for the child's grade level and the child's need in reading (e.g., in vocabulary and/or comprehension).

3. Keep the same reading goals for students with special needs as you have for the majority of students in your class. Instead of modifying goals, modify the instructional approach for students who need more targeted instruction. For example, if the students in your class are using a Story Impression for comprehension, add a sequential graphic organizer to the Story Impression for the student who needs more intense instruction.

4. Monitor the reading progress. See the assessment examples from the texts in this series. A simple checklist for sight words that you can add to and monitor on a chart is a good start.

5. Adapt instruction based on what you find in the progress monitoring.

In some RTI approaches, this process may be a first stage in a problem solving model (Bender & Shores, 2007). When students do not respond to targeted interventions in the classroom, they enter stage two. In stage two, a building level team may review the classroom data, consider other risk factors, and adjust the interventions or make a referral to stage three, or the stage where a disability is suspected and there is a referral for an evaluation for special education.

New Literacies and Culturally Responsive Instruction

What Are New Literacies?

Throughout this book, we have highlighted principles of CRI that include attention to students' background knowledge and experiences (i.e., their culture), how students respond to text using multiple learning styles or modalities (e.g., speaking, writing, drawing), and using multiple text types (i.e., going beyond traditional print texts to include image, sound, and interactive texts). Like CRI, 21st century perspectives of literacy focus on who students are, what they do, and how they learn—and bring these elements into the curriculum.

What is "new" about new literacies? Some 30 years before the new millennium, discussions about literacy began to change from reading as the process of decoding and encoding text, or a more psychological approach, to reading as the process of understanding and extending environmental print and other signs and symbols in the world, or a sociocultural approach (Lankshear & Knobel, 2006). From a new literacies perspective, we can make sense of the literacy experience only if we understand reading and writing "in the contexts of social, cultural, political, economic, historical practices to which they are integral, of which they are part" (Lankshear & Knobel, 2007, p. 1). Culturally, for example, groups that are oppressed use special symbolic systems for communication (e.g., gang symbols, the printing of books as a political threat in 17th-century England), and historically, communication before the printing press relied on symbolic and gestural systems (Kress, 2003; Leu, Kinzer, Coiro, & Cammack, 2004).

New literacies research takes these contexts into account. In one study, Orellana and Hernandez (1999) took groups of children on walks in central Los Angeles, where children read urban graffiti, posters and advertisements, sidewalk writing, and parking signs. The children "read the world," rather than the words. ELLs shared what they could read and what they could not understand, and their peers helped them make connections between the English words and words from their native language. Children visited stores and local landmarks, and they took pictures that contained images and words. Once in the classroom, they wrote stories to accompany their photos, made their own environmental signs, and wrote letters to their families.

Orellana and Hernandez's tour of a print-rich environment represents the sociocultural perspective of literacy—a foundation for new literacies practice. It may not be surprising that the tour not only reflected signs and symbols from a new literacies perspective, but also reflected CRI principles that you learned in this book: The students activated their background knowledge and experiences (their cultures), read multiple texts that were print and image, and engaged in multimodal response while on the tour and upon returning to the classroom. New literacies and CRI are certainly closely related, and they both focus on learners in the 21st century.

Who Are 21st Century Learners?

New literacies researchers emphasize that children live in an increasingly screen-dominant world, where their daily lives are spent in front of texts that are image, sound, and interactive; national studies reflect this increase in youth technology use. The latest Kaiser Family Foundation study (Rideout, Foehr, & Roberts, 2010) reflects this image-governed world, with 70% of youth ages 8–18 having a television in their bedroom and 50% having a game console in their bedroom.

However, technology use has greatly expanded beyond television and gaming, to online social networking, music, and mobile phone use, making total media exposure per day almost 12 hours for children ages 11–14 and almost 8 hours for 8- to 10-year-olds.

Daily teen texting has risen from 38% to 54% from February of 2008 to September 2009, with 1 in 30 teens sending more than 100 text messages per day (Lenhart, Ling, Campbell, & Purcell, 2010).

One question you may ask is whether media exposure and use are the same for diverse students. What about the "digital divide," a term associated with limited computer access for low-income students? We asked local teachers with a variety of cultures in their classrooms this question. Shellie Hamrick, a teacher licensed in elementary education and mild/moderate intervention with 10 years of urban school district experience, told us about her middle school students' computer and mobile phone use:

> On the computer they mostly listen to music and watch movies (bootlegs) on filmhill.com. They look at pictures of famous people or play games and try to get around the blocks set up in hopes to check their MySpace page. MySpace is huge! And YouTube. They text with text lingo, then they try to use that lingo in all of their writing (it's not gr8)! They text each other funny forwards and pictures; some just use their phones to play music and tell the time because they usually don't have any minutes on their prepay plans. . . . and they are interested in anything digital. My iPhone is so cool to them!

Social networking; computer use for music, movies, and games; and mobile phones for music and communication are in these students' daily lives. boyd (2007) found in her research that race and social class had little to do with access to social media sites—"poor black teens appear to be just as likely to join the site as white teens from wealthier backgrounds" (p. 121)—and concluded that, like shopping malls of the past, online social networks are places where teens go to socialize, as Hamrick shared with her example of students intent on accessing MySpace. boyd also found a difference in the social networking sites among socioeconomic class, with lower-income youth on MySpace and middle- and higher-income youth flocking to Facebook as it dramatically increased in popularity in 2009.

National research also shows an increase in computer use and mobile phone use for diverse students. The 2010 Kaiser Family Foundation study (Rideout et al., 2010), focusing on students ages 8–18, concluded that black and Hispanic children consume approximately 13 hours of media a day, about 4½ hours a day more than do white children, a difference that has grown from just over 2 hours in 2004. And diverse teens are using their cell phones to go online: 44% of black teens and 35% of Hispanic teens use their cell phones to go online, compared with 21% of white teens (Lenhart et al., 2010).

These studies focus on students from age 8, but younger children are no different. Rosen's (2010) research found that 35% of those ages 6 months to 3 years have a TV in their bedroom, 10% of those ages 4–8 have a computer in their bedroom, and 51% of those ages 9–12 have a mobile phone. Rosen adds—based on the average of four students per computer in our nation's schools (U.S. Census Bureau, 2006) and 25% of the population being under 18 years of age (U.S. Census Bureau, 2008)—that "the problem lies not in the number of computers, but rather how they are being used" (p. 3). Twenty-first century learners, whether considered "diverse" or not, are in the screen-dominant, technology-driven world.

What Do 21st Century Learners Need?

From a new literacies perspective, just as from a CRI perspective, 21st-century students need learning-centered instruction that brings their culture into the curriculum. Au (2007) notes that the culture in CRI is not only that of the local community, but also that of the *world* community. Technology is essential for 21st-century learning. It is global and has a focus on participation, connections with multiple learning modes (e.g., visual, auditory), and use of multiple forms of text beyond just print. These learners also need a particular perspective from their teachers. Says Sarah Brown Wessling, 2010 National Teacher of the Year: "We need 21st century teachers, not just adults teaching in the 21st century" (Teacher of the Year, 2010, p. 12). Twenty-first-century teachers can create the new literacies and culturally responsive conditions under which 21st-century learners will flourish.

New Literacies Instructional Strategies

Notice that new literacies instructional strategies build from the instructional principles for CRI. Recall that children need cultural connections with texts, participation, multimodal response to texts, and multiple types of texts. The bottom line is to leverage the technology available in order to personalize and feed the interest and energy of 21st-century students. Here are some suggestions to leverage this technology:

1. *Have students create products using technology.* In Chapter 3, we made suggestions about multimodal reading response that include making stories or comic strips that contain both image

and text. Use story creation as a foundation, and visit the comic creator and trading card sites on ReadWriteThink. You can also review comics created by students from the Center for Educational Pathways Comic Book Project, which began in an after-school program in New York City (http://www. comicbookproject.org; Bitz, 2004). Then have students expand their comic books to digital storytelling, which is creating a story using moving images, still images, voice, and sound (e.g., see the Center for Digital Story Telling at http://www.storycenter.org).

2. *Use virtual social networks in the classroom.* Some teachers are able to create private Facebook (http://www.facebook.com) groups for their students or parents or to use an educational social networking site with learning management functions like Schoolology: Your Digital Classroom (https://www.schoology.com). Others utilize popular social networking sites for children like Club Penguin (http://www.clubpenguin.com), a creative site for children with built-in player safety, citizenship, filtered chat, and live moderators. Mixbook (http://www.mixbook.com) is a site where students can create a book and invite friends to read it. Classroom blogs through EduBlog or Blogger can also be sites for student journaling and commenting in response to each other's posts. All these are easily connected to reading activities.

3. *Find ways to utilize digital devices.* Orellana and Hernandez (1999), in their environment walk with students described above, used digital cameras to capture the signs in the community. Digital cameras can be used in a number of ways—as a tool not just for digital storytelling (as in the suggestion above), but also for teaching. For example, as a teaching tool a teacher can attach the camera to an LCD projector in the classroom and display student work for real-time models and teaching moments as the work is projected to the front of the room. Mobile phones can also be used for photos, and teachers have incorporated texting with sites like Poll Everywhere (http://www.polleverywhere.com), an audience response system where teachers enter questions and students select the answer by using their mobile phones.

4. *Teach students to evaluate websites and other visual media.* Annenberg Media's site Teaching Reading 3-5: Research-Based Principles and Practices includes a New Literacies of the Internet Workshop (http://www.learner.org/workshops/teachreading35/

session5/index.html), which uses these three questions to evaluate websites:

a. Who created the information on this site?
b. What is the purpose of this site?
c. When was the information at this site updated?

Evaluation questions about both websites and other visual media can also be divided in a slightly different way: questions that ask about who created the message (i.e., the author of the message), what is in the message (e.g., colors, sounds, or print), and what is the meaning that the reader, or the receiver of the message, gets. Hobbs (1996) words the questions this way:

1. Who is creating the message, and who is consuming it?

2. What is the message being sent, and what is the meaning the reader is receiving?

3. What is represented by the image, and what is the reality the reader brings to that image?

You can find a collection of additional media evaluation questions in Pailliotet, Semali, Rodenberg, Giles, and Macaul's (2000) article on media literacy.

The Federal Trade Commission has also responded to this need for media literacy by launching a site called Admongo (http://www.admongo.gov), which targets children ages 8–12. Admongo is a game with the goal of raising awareness of advertising and marketing messages and with a focus on critical literacy. To play, children answer three basic media literacy questions, not unlike the ones you just read above:

a. Who is responsible for the ad?
b. What is the ad actually saying?
c. What does the ad want me to do?

Conclusion

In his essay "The Politics of Ignorance," Smith (1983) said: "Teachers do not ask the right kind of questions. Instead of inquiring what they should *do*, which can never be answered with the generality they expect, they should ask what they need to *know* in order to decide for themselves" (p. 3).

It would be impossible for us to answer all the questions you might have about the various cultures you will encounter among your students. Likewise, we just scratched the surface with information on new literacies and culturally diverse students with special needs. However, we hope you and your colleagues can use the information in this chapter to help you ask what you need to *know* in order to decide what you should *do* for all cultures represented in your classroom, what you should *do* with new literacies in the context of CRI, and what you should *do* for your diverse students with special needs. The remainder of the book will provide you with additional resources to support those decisions.

Professional Development

ACED: Analysis, Clarification, Extension, Discussion

I. REFLECTION (10–15 minutes)

ANALYSIS

- What, for you, were the most interesting and/or important ideas in this chapter?

  _____

  _____

  _____

  _____

- What new insights did you gain regarding the special populations or topics in this chapter that you did not already know?

  _____

  _____

  _____

  _____

CLARIFICATION

- Did anything surprise you? Confuse you?

  _____

  _____

  _____

  _____

- What clarifications do you need in order to better understand the populations or topics in this chapter?

  _____

  _____

  _____

  _____

- What barriers do you face when you have an ELL student whose language you do not speak? How do you deal with those barriers?

_____

_____

_____

_____

- If you teach early childhood Latino/a students, what have you observed about their social preparedness for school?

_____

_____

_____

_____

- How might the information presented in this chapter be applied in your own teaching situation?

_____

_____

_____

_____

II. DISCUSSION (30 minutes)

- Form groups of 4–6 members.
- Appoint a *facilitator (timer)* and *recorder.*
- Share responses. Make sure that each person has shared his or her responses to each category (Analysis/Clarification/ Extension).
- Help each other with any areas of confusion.
- Answer and/or discuss questions raised by group members.
- On chart paper, the recorder should summarize the main discussion points and identify issues or questions the group would like to raise for general discussion.

III. APPLICATION (10 minutes)

- Implement one of the instructional strategies from this chapter for ELLs in your classroom, and report the results to your discussion group.

_____

_____

_____

_____

- Implement one of the instructional strategies from this chapter for Latino/a students in your classroom, and report the results to your discussion group.

_____

_____

_____

_____

CHAPTER 5

Resources

107

*I*n this final chapter, we offer resources for classroom activities and for your own further learning. Both web-based and print resources are provided. (*Note:* Websites were all active as of October 2010.)

The resources are organized into highlighted ideas found in this book. First, we include web and print resources for culturally responsive instruction (CRI). Second, with English Language Learners (ELLs) spotlighted in each chapter in this book, we offer further teacher resource websites and books. Third, we list teacher resource websites and print texts for vocabulary and comprehension. The final section is multitextual materials, which lists print, audio, video, and interactive text resources for culturally responsive materials for your classroom.

Culturally Responsive Instruction

Teacher Resource Websites

About Día

http://www.ala.org/ala/mgrps/divs/alsc/initiatives/diadelosninos/aboutdia/aboutdia.cfm

Children's Day/Book Day, also known as El día de los niños/El día de los libros (Día), is a celebration of children, families, and reading held annually on April 30. The celebration emphasizes the importance of literacy for children of all linguistic and cultural backgrounds.

Annual National African American Read-In

http://www.ncte.org/action/aari

Join over a million readers in this event sponsored by the Black Caucus of the National Council of Teachers of English (NCTE) and by NCTE. The program has also been endorsed by the International Reading Association.

Geneva Gay

http://video.google.com/videoplay?docid=-601752990473453204#
Watch an online video with CRI specialist Geneva Gay.

International Reading Association

http://apps.reading.org/search/svc/submitquery?query=culturally+responsive+instruction&advanced=1

At the *International Reading Association (IRA)* website, you will find numerous documents on CRI.

Multicultural Review

http://www.mcreview.com

You may subscribe to the printed version, online version, or both. The Multicultural Review *publishes lists of recommended books, films, and videos on a wide variety of ethnic groups, such as Hmong, Thai, Laotians, Cambodians, Vietnamese, and Filipinos as well as African Americans, Mexican Americans, Jewish Americans, Chinese Americans, Puerto Ricans, and others.*

National Center for Education Statistics

http://nces.ed.gov

The U.S. Department of Education's Institute for Education Sciences *is home to the* National Center for Education Statistics, *which publishes the* National Assessment *of Educational Progress (NAEP), often known as the "Nation's Report Card." The NAEP data explorer allows users to generate tables based on fourth-, eighth-, and twelfth-grade standardized tests, disaggregated by a variety of student populations. You can also locate demographics on U.S. students.*

Teachers College Press

http://www.teacherscollegepress.com/multicultural education.html

At this website, you will find individual titles of books from the Multicultural Education Series edited by James Banks.

Print Resources

Bishop, R. S. (1992). Children's books in a multicultural world: A view from the USA. In E. Evans (Ed.), *Reading against racism* (pp. 19–38). Buckingham, England: Open University Press.

Irvine, J. J., & Armento, B. J. (2001). *Culturally responsive teaching: Lesson planning for elementary and middle grades.* Boston, MA: McGraw-Hill.

Janks, H. (2010). *Literacy and power.* New York, NY: Routledge.

Nuri Robins, K., Lindsey, R. B., Lindsey, D. B., & Terrell, R. D (2006). *Culturally proficient instruction: A guide for people who teach* (2nd ed.). Thousand Oaks, CA: Corwin Press.

Redman, G. L. (2007). *A casebook for exploring diversity* (3rd ed.). Upper Saddle River, NJ: Prentice Hall.

Singleton, G. E., & Linton, C. (2006). *Courageous conversations about race: A field guide for achieving equity in the schools.* Thousand Oaks, CA: Corwin Press.

English Language Learners

Teacher Resource Websites

Colorin' Colorado

http://www.colorincolorado.org

Teachers who work with English as a Second Language (ESL) learners will find children's books, stories, activities, and strategies to help preK–3, 4–8, and 9–12 students learn to read. The site has teamed up with Reading Rockets and the American Federation of Teachers. There is also a wealth of resources for families, including a Spanish-language newsletter.

Dave's ESL Café

http://www.daveseslcafe.com

The website is divided into Stuff for Teachers (e.g., classroom ideas and teacher forums), Stuff for Students (e.g., grammar lessons, quizzes, and student forums), and Stuff for Everyone (e.g., podcasts, photo gallery, and chats).

Double the Work: Challenges and Solutions to Acquiring Language and Academic Literacy for Adolescent English Language Learner

http://www.all4ed.org/publications/DoubleWork/DoubleWork.pdf

This report was published in January 2007 by the Alliance for Excellent Education.

ELL Resource: Interesting Things for ESL Students

http://www.manythings.org

This website contains loads of word games, puzzles, quizzes, exercises, slang, and proverbs for ELLs to use to practice vocabulary, sentence construction, grammar, listening, and pronunciation. All the exercises are self-scoring, and students get immediate feedback.

English as Second Language

http://www.rong-chang.com

This website provides links to dozens of other sites, including, but not limited to, ESL podcasts, reading lessons for ELLs, writing lessons for ELLs, a dictionary of idioms, and games.

English Daily

http://www.englishdaily626.com

At this website, students can practice English with video grammar lessons and exercises that help them listen, speak, and write.

ESL Printables

http://www.eslprintables.com

This is a website where ELL teachers exchange resources like worksheets, lesson plans, and activities.

International Children's Digital Library

http://www.childrenslibrary.org

This website provides over 4,000 books in 54 languages. Books can be viewed in their entirety and can be searched using different categories, such as age, genre, and award winners.

National Clearinghouse for English Language Acquisition & Language Instruction Educational Programs

http://www.ncela.gwu.edu

The clearinghouse collects, coordinates, and conveys a broad range of research and resources in support of an inclusive approach to high-quality education for ELLs.

National Council of Teachers of English Position Paper on the Role of English Teachers in Educating English Language Learners (ELLs)

http://www.ncte.org/positions/statements/teacherseducatingell

This paper from the NCTE gives pointers on how teachers can help ELLs both learn and work in English, while retaining their heritage languages.

Pathways for Teaching and Learning with English Language Learners

http://www.ncte.org/pathways/ell

This yearlong professional development program is intended to support middle and secondary mainstream teachers across the disciplines as they work to raise achievement among ELLs.

The Literacy List

http://home.comcast.net/~djrosen/litlist/esolwebsites.html

This website includes a list of various websites addressing ELL issues.

Print Resources

Jesness, J. (2004). *Teaching English language learners K–12: A quick start guide for the new teacher*. Thousand Oaks, CA: Corwin Press.

Linan-Thompson, S., & Vaughn, S. (2007). *Research-based methods of reading instruction for English language learners*. Alexandria, VA: Association for Supervision and Curriculum Development.

McIntyre, E., Kyle, D. W., Chen, C-T., Kraemer, J., & Parr, J. (2009). *6 principles for teaching English language learners in all classrooms.* Thousand Oaks, CA: Corwin Press.

Vocabulary and Comprehension

Teacher Resource Websites

Eduplace

http://www.eduplace.com/graphicorganizer/index.jsp

This website has hundreds of graphic organizers with text also in Spanish.

Ed Helper

http://www.edhelper.com/teachers/graphic_organizers.htm EdHelper.com

This website has dozens of free blank downloadable graphic organizers.

Freeology

http://freeology.com/graphicorgs/index.php

Here, you will find nearly 100 free printable graphic organizers for all occasions. A thumbnail gallery shows you the file before you click it.

Scholastic's Graphic Organizers

http://teacher.scholastic.com/lessonplans/graphicorg/index.htm

Scholastic offers free graphic organizers categorized by organizer patterns, reading comprehension, story elements, and assessment.

Super Teacher Worksheets

http://www.superteacherworksheets.com/graphic-organizers.html

Free story webs, writing hamburger, Venn diagrams, story maps, concept maps, t-charts, and more.

TeacherVision

http://www.teachervision.fen.com/graphic-organizers/printable/6293.html?s2

This collection of free, ready-to-use graphic organizers is designed to facilitate understanding of key concepts by allowing students to visually identify key points and ideas.

ReadWriteThink

http://www.readwritethink.org

This website is jointly sponsored by NCTE and IRA. You will find literacy lesson plans, printouts, and parent resources.

Print Resources

Beck, I. L., & McKeown, M. G. (2006). *Improving comprehension with Questioning the Author.* New York: Scholastic.

Block, C. C., Gambrell, L., & Pressley, M. (Eds.). (2002). *Improving reading comprehension: Rethinking research, theory, and classroom practice.* San Francisco: Jossey-Bass.

Block, C. C., & Pressley, M. (Eds.). (2001). *Comprehension instruction: Research-based best practices.* New York: Guilford Press.

Daniels, H. (1994). *Literature circles: Voice and choice in the student-centered classroom.* Portland, ME: Stenhouse.

Day, J. P., Spiegel, D. I., McLellan, J., & Brown, V. B. (2002). *Moving forward with literature circles.* New York: Scholastic.

Harvey, S. (1998). *Nonfiction matters: Reading, writing, and research in grades 3–8.* Portland, ME: Stenhouse.

Harvey, S., & Goudvis, A. (2000). *Strategies that work.* Portland, ME: Stenhouse.

Hoyt, L. (1998). *Revisit, reflect, retell: Strategies for improving reading comprehension.* Portsmouth, NH: Heinemann.

Koskinen, P. S., Blum, I. H., Bisson, S. A., Phillips, S. M., Creamer, T. S., & Baker, T. K. (1999). Shared reading, books, and audiotapes: Supporting diverse students in school and at home. *The Reading Teacher, 52,* 430–444.

Martinez, M., & Roser, N. (1985). Read it again: The value of repeated readings during storytime. *The Reading Teacher, 38,* 782–786.

McLaughlin, M. (2003). *Guided comprehension in the primary grades.* Newark, DE: International Reading Association.

McLaughlin, M., & Allen, M. B. (2002). *Guided comprehension in action: A teaching model for grades 3–8.* Newark, DE: International Reading Association.

McLaughlin, M., & DeVoogd, G. (2004). *Critical literacy: Enhancing students' comprehension of text.* New York: Scholastic.

Miller, D. (2002). *Reading with meaning: Teaching comprehension in the primary grades.* Portland, ME: Stenhouse.

Opitz, M. F., & Rasinski, T. V. (2008). *Good-bye round robin: 25 effective oral reading strategies* (Updated ed.). Portsmouth, NH: Heinemann.

Padak, N., & Rasinski, T. (2008). The games children play. *The Reading Teacher, 62,* 363–365.

Perfect, K. A. (1999). Rhyme and reason: Poetry for the heart and head. *The Reading Teacher, 52*, 728–737.

Prescott, J. O. (2003). The power of reader's theater. *Instructor, 112*(5), 22–26.

Rasinski, T. V. (2010). *The fluent reader: Oral reading strategies for building word recognition, fluency, and comprehension* (2nd ed.). New York: Scholastic.

Rasinski, T. V., & Hoffman, J. V. (2003). Theory and research into practice: Oral reading in the school literacy curriculum. *Reading Research Quarterly, 38*, 510–522.

Rasinski, T. V., & Padak, N. (2008). *From phonics to fluency: Effective teaching of decoding and reading fluency in the elementary school* (2nd ed.). New York: Longman.

Rasinski, T. V., Padak, N. D., Church, B. W., Fawcett, G., Hendershop, J., Henry, J., . . . Roskos, K. A. (Eds.). (2000). *Teaching comprehension and exploring multiple literacies: Strategies from* The Reading Teacher. Newark, DE: International Reading Association.

Rasinski, T. V., Padak, N., & Fawcett, G. (2010). *Teaching children who find reading difficult* (4th ed.). New York: Pearson.

Wilfong, L.G. (2008). Building fluency, word-recognition ability, and confidence in struggling readers: The Poetry Academy. *The Reading Teacher, 62*, 4–13.

Wilhelm, J. D. (1996). *You gotta BE the book: Teaching engaged and reflective reading with adolescents.* New York: Teachers College Press.

Wilhelm, J. D. (2001). *Improving comprehension with think-aloud strategies.* New York: Scholastic.

Wilhelm, J. D. (2002). *Action strategies for deepening comprehension: Role plays, text structure, tableaux, talking statues, and other enrichment techniques that engage students with text.* New York: Scholastic.

Wilhelm, J., Baker, T., & Dube, J. (2001). *Strategic reading: Guiding students to lifelong literacy.* Portsmouth, NH: Heinemann.

Multitextual Materials

Websites with Multicultural Book Listings

In Chapter 2, we included a checklist for assessing the content of culturally responsive materials. The checklist contains the domains of overall literary quality, cultural characters, cultural setting, cultural authenticity, and cultural illustrations. The following links help you find books that meet these quality domains.

American Library Association's Coretta Scott King Book Awards

http://www.ala.org/ala/mgrps/rts/emiert/cskbookawards/recipients.cfm

This site provides the Coretta Scott King award recipients from 1970 to the present, along with other resources from the book publishers as well as links to other Multicultural Awards from the American Library Association.

International Children's Digital Library

http://www.childrenslibrary.org

This site provides over 4,000 books in 54 languages. Books can be viewed in their entirety and can be searched using different categories, such as age, genre, and award winners.

Reading Is Fundamental

http://www.rif.org/us/search.htm?search=multicultural&x=11&y=8

On this site, Reading Is Fundamental lays out 100 of the decade's best multicultural reads for prekindergarten through grade 8.

Scholastic's How to Choose the Best Multicultural Books

http://www2.scholastic.com/browse/article.jsp?id=3757

Instructor authors Clegg, Miller, Vanderhoof, Ramirez, and Ford offer reviews of multicultural children's books for grades K–8, advice from children's authors, key criteria when selecting books, and a list of notable multicultural authors.

Websites with Graphic Novels

Graphic novels are books that combine both print and image text. Like print texts, they are organized in multiple genres (e.g., classics, biographies, children, teen), as shown in the websites about graphic novels below. We discussed Telgemeier's graphic adaptation of Ann Martin's *Baby-Sitter's Club* series (e.g., *The Truth About Stacy*, Telgemeier, 2006a; *Kristy's Great Idea*, Telgemeier, 2006b) in Chapter 3 as a way to bring multimodality to Narrow Reading, a strategy that involves reading multiple texts by the same author. Children who are new to graphic novels may enjoy the varied short story anthologies edited by Pulitzer Prize–winning graphic novelist Art Speigelman and Francoise Mouly (e.g., *Little Lit: Folklore and Fairytale Funnies*, 2000; *Big Fat Little Lit*, 2006; *The TOON Treasury of Classic Children's Comics*, 2009).

Graphic Novel Reporter's Core List

http://www.graphicnovelreporter.com/content/core-list-essential-graphic-novels-and-manga-booksellers-feature-stories

The Core List of Essential Graphic Novels for Booksellers from the Graphic Novel Reporter has an adults', teens', and children's lists.

Scott McCloud's Blog

http://scottmccloud.com

Scott McCloud, who wrote the popular informational graphic novels Understanding Comics *(1994),* Reinventing Comics *(2000), and* Making Comics *(2006), keeps a blog about webcomics, print comics, inventions, and his presentations and consulting with schools.*

The University of Buffalo Libraries

http://library.buffalo.edu/libraries/asl/guides/graphicnovels/genres

This page from the University of Buffalo Libraries website lists graphic novels within superhero, fantasy, horror/supernatural, science fiction, humor, manga, and other genres.

The Young Adult Library Services Association

http://www.ala.org/ala/mgrps/divs/yalsa/booklistsawards/greatgraphicnovelsforteens/gn.cfm

The Young Adult Library Services Association (YALSA) site lists great graphic novels for teens and the top 10 great graphic novels for teens from 2007 to the present. Students can also nominate their favorites.

Toon Books

http://toon-books.com

Authors Mouly and Speigelman direct and advise Toon Books, a site that lists a collection of high-quality comics for children ages 4 and up.

Websites with Audio Content

Folk Songs and Songs of America

http://www.contemplator.com/america
http://www.scoutsongs.com/categories/patriotic.html

Jazz Chants

Jazz chants offer a rhythmic expression of standard American English as it occurs in situational contexts. The following are a few examples:

Graham, C. (1986). *Small talk.* New York: Oxford University Press.
Graham, C. (1988). *Jazz chant fairy tales.* New York: Oxford University Press.

Graham, C. (1994). *Mother Goose jazz chants*. New York: Oxford University Press.

Graham, C. (2000). *Jazz chants old and new*. New York: Oxford University Press.

Songs for Children

http://judyanddavid.com/cma.html
http://www.bussongs.com
http://www.theteachersguide.com/ChildrensSongs.htm
http://www.niehs.nih.gov/kids/music.htm
http://www.niehs.nih.gov/kids/music.htm#index
http://www.head-start.lane.or.us/education/activities/music/index.html
http://www.kididdles.com
http://www.songsforteaching.com
http://www.jmeacham.com/calendar/calendar.songs.poems.htm (calendar songs and poems)
http://www.fpx.de/fp/Disney/Lyrics

Speeches, Audiobooks, and Podcasts

Audible

http://www.audible.com

Audible is an Amazon company that contains audiobooks (with categories for, e.g., kids, classics, fiction, and teens) and other audio entertainment like comedy, newspapers and magazines, nostalgia radio, and tv. Fees are charged monthly or annually.

Books Should Be Free.com

http://www.booksshouldbefree.com

BooksShouldBeFree.com draws from public domain sources (e.g., Gutenburg.org, which digitizes books, and Librivox.org, which records books) to deliver free audio books. Popular genres on the site are Top 100, children, fiction, fantasy, and mystery.

Internet Archive

http://www.archive.org

The Internet Archive is a member of the American Library Association and works in collaboration with the Library of Congress and the Smithsonian Institution. Its website includes texts, audio, moving images, software, and archived webpages, with the purpose of offering permanent free access to the public. Its audio archive is an audio and MP3 library containing over 200,000 free digital recordings (e.g., books, poetry, music, news).

iTunes Podcasts

http://www.apple.com/itunes/podcasts

With free iTunes software downloaded on a computer, users can follow these tips from Apple in searching, finding, playing, saving, and creating podcast playlists. There are also tutorials for creating podcasts.

Flocabulary: Hip Hop in the Classroom

http://www.flocabulary.com

Flocabulary has free teacher resources and tips on how to rap and produces free educational hip-hop music to teach vocabulary, reading, writing, social studies, math, and science in grades 3–12. Flocabulary also produces The Week in Rap (theweekinrap.com), which contains rap videos about the week's news.

National Public Radio Podcasts

http://www.npr.org/rss/podcast/podcast_directory.php

This site is the directory of free National Public Radio podcasts, searchable by topic (e.g., books, arts and life, health, U.S., world), title, or news provider. Podcasts can be downloaded, and users can also subscribe to particular podcasts using the directory linked with iTunes or Yahoo.

Political Speeches from Wake Forest University

http://www.wfu.edu/~louden/Political%20Communication/Class%20Information/SPEECHES.html

Allen Louden of Wake Forest University created this site, which includes links to collections of political speeches, individual presidential sites, and other audio sites and speech collections.

Websites with Video Content

Annenberg Media

http://www.learner.org

Annenberg Media has a host of teacher professional development resources as well as teacher resources in the arts, foreign languages, literature and language arts, mathematics, science, and social studies and history. Browse by grade bands that include K–4 and 4–8.

Beat Boppers

http://www.beatboppers.com

Beat Boppers creates downloadable music for early childhood and early elementary grades. Beat Boppers' YouTube channel has music videos that students can watch or actively engage in, while also watching the words and images.

Ignite Learning

http://www.ignitelearning.com

Ignite Learning produces educational videos for grades 4 through 8. It also has a YouTube channel for easy viewing of its short videos on specific topics (e.g., molecules, seasons, volcanic eruptions).

PBS Kids

http://pbskids.org/video

PBS Kids has videos in a variety of categories like creative arts, health, holidays, language and literacy, mathematics, science, and social and environmental growth.

TeacherTube

http://www.teachertube.com

TeacherTube is an online community for sharing instructional videos. Available along with videos are documents, audio and photo content, and blogs. TeacherTube recently partnered with Pearson Education to provide further teaching resources through TeacherVision, a site with K–12 tools and resources.

YouTube EDU

http://www.youtube.com/education?b=400

YouTube, the most popular video site, contains many educational channels and videos that can be used for vocabulary, comprehension, and specific content areas. But there is also YouTube EDU, which hosts channels like Universities (e.g., The Open University, Stanford University, and Emory University) and categorizes videos by topics like business, education, history, mathematics, and science.

Interactive Websites

These websites are a mix of interactive, audio, and visual texts where students and teachers can create, share, and engage in online content. The sites are all free. Many are social and include games that can also be useful on a classroom interactive whiteboard (e.g., Smart or Promethean Board).

Bubbabrain

http://www.bubbabrain.com

Teachers can generate or use existing study games in vocabulary and the content areas.

Draw Anywhere

http://www.drawanywhere.com

Students can create concept maps and diagrams online and collaborate. The free basic membership includes three diagrams, up to 10MB storage, and team collaboration.

Edublogs

http://edublogs.org

Teachers and students can create blogs with customized designs and options to include videos, photos, and podcasts.

Language Link

http://www.oup.com/elt/global/products/happyearth/eagle

At this site from Oxford University Press, students can learn vocabulary through activities like writing words that they hear or choosing words with associated images that describe a sentence.

Mixbook

http://www.mixbook.com

Mixbook is a place where students can create books, share them with friends, upload photos, and mix their books with special features. Books can be bound and delivered.

Quizlet

http://quizlet.com

Students can study vocabulary or content areas, create their own flashcards or share flashcard sets with other users. Students can enter teams, log scores, and hold discussions.

RIF Reading Activities

http://www.rif.org/us/literacy-resources/activities.htm

This site contains activities by Reading Is Fundamental. Children can make personalized stories, send postcards, build word search puzzles, publish book reviews, build stories with story starters, and enter words to create poetry.

Scratch

http://scratch.mit.edu

Created at the Massachusetts Institute of Technology Media Lab, Scratch is a place where students can create their own interactive stories, animations, games, music, and art and share their creations on the web.

StudyStack

http://www.studystack.com

Teachers can generate or use existing flashcard, crossword, matching, word search, and hangman activities for vocabulary words.

Shelfari

http://www.shelfari.com

Students can build virtual bookshelves, discover popular books with their friends, discuss books online, discover and learn from peers with similar reading tastes, and participate in online book groups.

The Neverending Tale

http://www.coder.com/creations/tale/stacks.html

Students can add to story threads with guidelines for voice, creativity, and proper English grammar and spelling.

Vocabulary University

http://www.myvocabulary.com

Myvocabulary.com provides sessions with grade-level-appropriate words used in context. Activities include fill-in-the-blank, definition match, synonym/antonym encounter, crossword, word find/search, true or false sentences, contextual stories (including an audio recording), and concentration puzzles.

Wacky Web Tails

http://www.eduplace.com/tales

On this site by Houghton Mifflin's Eduplace, students can build their own stories by entering places, adjectives, verbs, and nouns.

Word Central

http://www.wordcentral.com/games.html

Brought to you by Merriam-Webster, this site enables students to build a dictionary and play games to build vocabulary.

Wordia

http://www.wordia.com

Wordia is a visual dictionary of words that includes a word of the day, games, a calendar, and a blog. Students can upload their own videos about words or watch videos from others in the Wordia community.

Wordle

http://www.wordle.net

Students can generate word clouds to reflect books, word walls, or any reading topics.

Book Club Ideas

Book Club

Throughout the book, you have seen icons indicating activities or discussion points that lend themselves to book club conversations. We hope you and your colleagues will take advantage of these opportunities. Our experience has taught us that learning from and with each other is a powerful way to promote innovation. In this appendix, we provide additional questions and ideas for discussion. They are organized according to the chapters in the book.

Chapter 1: Culturally Responsive Instruction: Definitions, Research, and Considerations

- Create a bulleted list of what you think fellow teachers should know about culturally responsive instruction. Discuss the list with your principal.
- In this chapter, we talked about the importance of reflection. Donald Schon, author of the groundbreaking book *The Reflective Practitioner: How Professionals Think in Action* (published by Basic Books in 1984), focuses more on reflection *in* action than on reflection *on* action. What is the difference? How do you reflect *in* action with your culturally diverse students?

Book Club

- Work with one of your students to create a Venn diagram comparing and contrasting your cultural background with that of your student. What did you learn? How can you use that information?

- Think back to the beginning of your teaching career. What were you taught about working with diverse students? Share these insights with colleagues and together attempt to determine what advice is still appropriate and what, if anything, needs to be changed.

- Brainstorm with colleagues: What does it mean to be *responsive* to student cultures?

- In this chapter, we introduced Banks' six elements of culture: (1) values and behavioral styles; (2) language and dialects; (3) nonverbal communications; (4) cultural cognitiveness; (5) perspectives, worldviews, and frames of reference; and (6) identification. What does each of these mean? How do you connect these elements to your culture? To that of your students?

Chapter 2: Assessing Reading Instruction for Cultural Responsiveness

- Describe how a lesson you teach would look if you were using backward design.

- Do you have any "kids from chaos"? Tell your discussion group about one of them, and brainstorm together some ideas for meeting the student's literacy needs.

- Locate two books you could read to become informed about cultures different than your own. Read the books, and tell your group what you learned.

- Review the cultural interview described in this chapter and located in Appendix B. What questions are most important in finding out the interests of students in your classroom?

- List possible revisions to your classroom assessment plans. Then rank order these. Explain your reasoning to your colleagues.

- Discuss each "big idea" about assessment in more detail. Decide if you agree or disagree with each, why, and what implications the ideas have for your classroom assessment plans for culturally responsive instruction.

- Research indicates teachers of culturally and linguistically diverse students who excel as readers have sophisticated knowledge of reading instruction. Do a Jigsaw with the sophisticated knowledge among members of your discussion group. (see Jigsaw, p. 76) is a cooperative learning strategy developed in 1978 by Elliot Aronson and his students at the University of Texas and the University of California. The basic procedure in Jigsaw is to divide a topic into subtopics, one for each group member. The goal is for each member to (1) master the concepts in his or her subtopic and (2) develop a strategy for teaching these concepts to the other members.)

- With your discussion group, brainstorm a list of nonlinguistic ways for students to respond to their reading.

- Create a literacy I Have, Who Has game, and do it with your discussion group (see I Have Who Has, p. 57).

- For the Narrow Reading strategy, gather a list of narrative print texts and informational print texts with the same author to share with your discussion group. Do the same for audio and video texts.

- Brainstorm with your colleagues ways to enhance students' participation using peer activities.

- Create a list with your colleagues of online instructional tools that can be used in the classroom.

Chapter 4: Beyond Strategies

- Gather information on a cultural group not addressed in this book. Lead a discussion about what you learned with your group.

- Write your own literacy autobiography to share with your students, who will, in turn, write their own.

- Look through some standardized tests you administer for language or cultural barriers. Share them with your discussion group, and discuss how you could help students work through these barriers.

- Develop two or three ways that culturally responsive instruction and Response to Intervention are related instructional approaches. Share with your colleagues how you can interrelate them in your classroom.

- The section on new literacies describes 21st-century learners as living in a screen-dominant world with daily frequent technology use, including texting, watching online movies, and using mobile phones for surfing the web. With your colleagues, brainstorm the devices you see your students using, the popular culture texts they discuss, and the computer sites they frequent. What are the implications for bringing culture into the classroom?

- Review the chapter's suggested instructional strategies for new literacies. Select two strategies you believe would be useful and feasible for the students in your classroom. Make detailed plans for implementing these strategies in your classroom.

Chapter 5: Resources

- Work with colleagues to generate a list of more websites you could suggest to parents.

- With your colleagues, select a professional book from the list in this chapter. Start a new book club.

- Do a Jigsaw (see Jigsaw, p. 76) with the websites in this chapter.

- This chapter lists video websites where you and your students can search, select, and use videos as well as converting the videos to files. Plan steps for searching and using these sites for multitextual resources in your classroom.

- Review the list of websites for social networking. Notice that they include blogs, book sharing, and mapping. Select two or more sites that you can use for your instruction or for student learning. Describe the sites, and tell your colleagues how you will use them.

- Search the web for additional resources and sites that can provide support for culturally responsive instruction. Share these with your colleagues.

Cultural Interview

*C*onducting the Cultural Interview involves several steps that are based on the time you have available, the relationship you already have built with the student or group of students you will interview, and what information you want to know. See chapter 3 for details of 6 interview steps: (1) decide who you want to interview, (2) determine a purpose for your interview, (3) obtain informal permission for your interview, (4) choose interview questions, (5) determine the setting and materials for the interview, and (6) conduct the interview. In conducting the interview, notice that the questions begin with ones about what people the student interacts with at home and in the community. Information about particular people helps with probing for the activities questions. The activities questions are divided into questions about reading, computer use, music, games, and other activities. Probing questions are available to assist with gathering more information about the activities. Note that phrases like, "tell me more about that," and "what do you mean by . . . ?" also help to gain more information and clarify information given.

What people do you interact with at home and in the community?

- Who lives at home with you?
- Who comes to your house that does not live at home?
- With whom do you do things with outside of home?

At home (or at school), what do you **read**?

- What magazine?
- What newspaper?
- What book(s)?
- What types of magazines, newspapers, or books?
- What comics?

Follow-up questions for probing about the reading:

- With whom do you read?
- Which [magazine, newspaper, book, comic]?
- What section of the [magazine or newspaper]?
- When do you get the [magazine, newspaper, book, comic]?
- From where do you get the [magazine, newspaper, book, comic]?
- With whom do you talk about what you read?
- What do you like about _____?
- What do you dislike about _____?
- What do you look at more, the pictures or the words?
- What types of images are in the reading?

At home (and/or at school), what do you do on the **computer**?

- With whom do you use the computer?
- What instant message program do you use?
- What do you look for on the Internet?
- Do you use social networking sites, like Facebook or YouTube?
- What do you do on [the social networking site] (e.g., What do you upload? What friends are you connected with? What do you post as your status?)?
- With whom do you talk on the Internet?
- What Internet sites do you like?
- What software do you use?
- How often are you on the computer? What are you doing?

At home (and/or at school), what do you watch on **TV**?

- With whom do you watch TV?
- What TV stations?

- What TV shows?
- What DVDs? What movies?

Follow-up questions for probing about TV:

- What show did you like last year?
- What actor do you like?
- What superhero do you like? Why?
- What do you like about watching [show]?
- Can you explain what happens on the show/cartoon?
- What does the imagery/animation look like?
- What character do you like?
- What types of movies do you like to watch?
- What movies don't you like?
- What shows do others in your home like?

At home (and/or at school), what **music** do you listen to?

- What songs?
- What artists?
- Do you listen on the computer or another way?

Follow-up questions for probing about music:

- How many songs do you have on your iPod/MP3 player? (Favorite CDs? Radio station? When do you listen to it?)
- What is the last song that you listened to?
- What songs would you suggest to your friends?
- What do you like about [song/artist]?
- What song did you like a lot last year?

At home (and/or at school), what **games** do you play?

- What video games?
- What outdoor games?
- What sports?
- What trading cards?
- What board games?

Follow-up questions for probing about games:

- On what game system (e.g., Playstation, Xbox, Wii)?
- What game system do you like the best? Why?
- With whom do you play?

- What do you like about the game? What character do you like to be (for role-playing games)? Why?
- What are the goals of the game?
- What trading card game do you play?
- What character do you like? Why?
- Will you explain the different characters in the game?
- How many levels are there?
- With whom do you talk to about the game?
- What do you talk about?

At home (and/or at school), what other **activities** do you like to do (in addition to the activities you described in the previous categories of reading, computer, TV, music, and games)?

- What else do you read?
- What else do you do on the computer?
- What else do you watch on TV?
- What other music do you listen to?
- What other games do you play?

Follow-up questions for probing about other activities:

- With whom do you do [the activity]?
- Where do you do [the activity]?
- When do you do [the activity]?
- What do you like about [the activity]?
- What is different between [one activity] and [another activity]?
- Did you do [the activity] last year?

The Essential Primary Grade Sight Word List

We developed this list of 400 essential words from the high-frequency word lists created by Dolch (1955), Fry (1980), and Cunningham and Allington (1999). It also includes words that represent the most common phonograms (Fry, 1998) and words selected by primary-grade teachers as words every student should recognize by sight and know by the end of third grade. We recommend that primary-grade teachers in a school work together to determine the words that should be learned at each grade level. Kindergarten children might learn 25 words, and 125 words might be learned during each of the primary years—first, second, and third grade. The list could easily be covered in 25 weeks by presenting and teaching five words each week. There is no best way to teach these words. They should be put on the class word wall and practiced regularly. Students can add them to their personal word banks and use them for practice and word games. Class word games work well in teaching these words. It is also a good idea to send the words home at the beginning of the school year and ask parents to regularly work with their children in helping them learn to know and recognize the words. Because these are high-frequency words, the absolute best way to provide plenty of exposure to them is through regular and wide reading.

about	black	drum	good	job
above	blue	earth	got	jump
add	book	eat	grade	junk
after	both	eight	great	just
again	bottom	end	green	keep
air	boy	enough	group	kind
all	bring	even	grow	know
almost	brother	every	had	land
along	bug	example	hand	large
also	but	eye	hard	last
always	buy	face	has	later
am	by	fake	have	learn
America	call	family	he	leave
and	came	far	head	left
animal	can	farm	hear	let
another	can't	fast	help	letter
answer	car	father	her	life
any	carry	favorite	here	lip
are	cat	feed	hill	light
around	change	feet	him	like
as	chill	few	high	line
ask	children	find	his	list
at	city	first	hold	little
ate	clean	five	home	live
away	close	fly	hop	lock
back	cold	follow	hot	look
bag	come	food	house	long
bank	could	for	how	luck
be	country	found	hug	made
because	crab	four	hum	mail
bed	cut	friend	hurt	main
been	dad	from	I	make
before	day	full	idea	man
began	did	fun	if	many
begin	different	funny	important	map
being	do	gave	in	may
bell	does	get	into	me
below	done	girl	is	mean
best	don't	give	it	men
better	down	glow	its	might
between	draw	go	it's	mile
big	drink	goes	jam	mine

miss	over	seven	ten	want
mom	own	shall	than	warm
more	page	she	thank	was
most	paper	show	that	wash
mother	part	should	the	watch
mountain	people	shout	their	water
move	pick	sick	them	way
much	picture	side	then	we
must	place	sing	there	well
my	plant	sink	these	went
myself	play	sister	they	were
name	please	sit	they're	what
near	point	six	thing	when
need	pretty	sleep	think	where
new	pull	slow	this	which
never	put	small	those	while
next	ran	so	thought	white
new	read	some	three	who
nice	red	something	through	why
nine	really	sometimes	time	win
night	ride	song	to	will
no	right	soon	today	wish
not	river	sound	together	with
now	rock	spell	too	without
number	round	stand	took	write
of	run	start	top	wrong
off	said	state	tree	won't
often	same	still	try	word
old	saw	stop	turn	work
on	say	store	two	world
once	school	story	under	would
one	sea	study	until	write
only	second	such	up	year
open	see	take	upon	yellow
or	seed	talk	us	yes
other	seem	tap	use	you
our	sentence	teacher	very	young
out	set	tell	walk	your

Source: T. Rasinski, N. Padak, & G. Fawcett. (2010). *Teaching children who find reading difficult* (4th ed.). Boston: Pearson.

Graphic Organizer Templates

Vocabulary Mapping

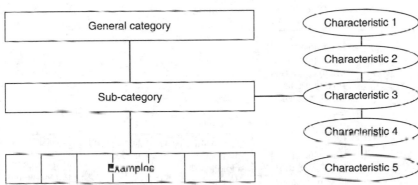

| General category |
| Sub-category |
| Examples |

- Characteristic 1
- Characteristic 2
- Characteristic 3
- Characteristic 4
- Characteristic 5

Example

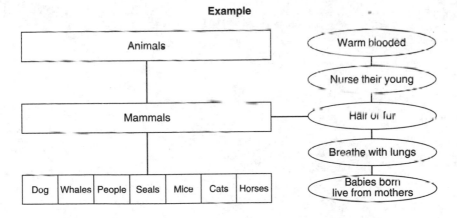

| Animals |
| Mammals |

| Dog | Whales | People | Seals | Mice | Cats | Horses |

- Warm blooded
- Nurse their young
- Hair or fur
- Breathe with lungs
- Babies born live from mothers

Story Mapping

Problem-Solution Structure

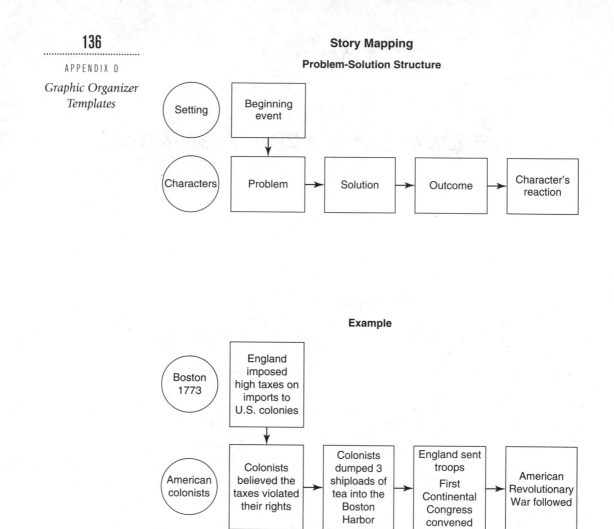

Example

Story Mapping

Cause-Effect Structure

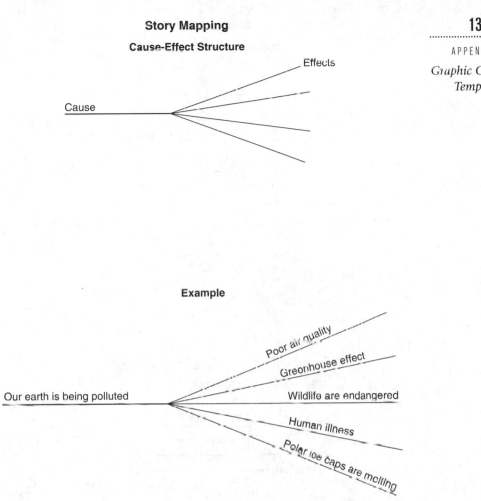

Effects

Cause

Example

Our earth is being polluted

Poor air quality

Greenhouse effect

Wildlife are endangered

Human illness

Polar ice caps are melting

Story Mapping

Compare-Contrast Structure

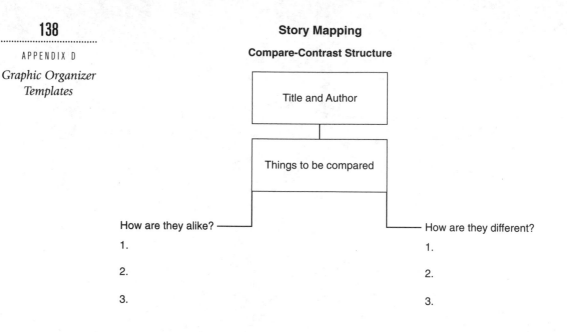

Title and Author

Things to be compared

How are they alike? ——
1.

2.

3.

—— How are they different?
1.

2.

3.

Example

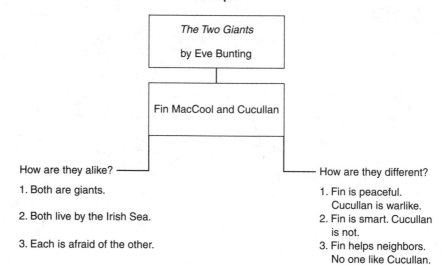

The Two Giants

by Eve Bunting

Fin MacCool and Cucullan

How are they alike? ——
1. Both are giants.

2. Both live by the Irish Sea.

3. Each is afraid of the other.

—— How are they different?
1. Fin is peaceful.
   Cucullan is warlike.
2. Fin is smart. Cucullan
   is not.
3. Fin helps neighbors.
   No one like Cucullan.

Decision Model

Problem–Solution Structure

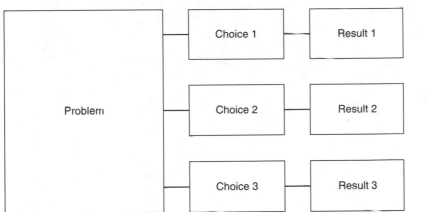

Example

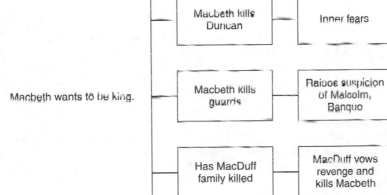

References

Allington, R. L. (2002). What I've learned about effective reading instruction. *Phi Delta Kappan, 83,* 740–747.

Anderson, R. C., & Freebody, P. (1981). Vocabulary knowledge. In J. Guthrie (Ed.), *Comprehension and teaching: Research reviews* (pp. 77–117). Newark, DE: International Reading Association.

Armstrong, T. (2009). *Multiple intelligences in the classroom* (3rd ed.). Alexandria, VA: Association for Supervision and Curriculum Development.

Aronson, E. (1978). *The jigsaw classroom.* Beverly Hills, CA: Sage.

Au, K. H. (2001). Culturally responsive instruction as a dimension of new literacies. *Reading Online, 5*(1). Available at http://www.readingonline.org/newliteracies/lit_index.asp?HREF=/newliteracies/xu/index.html

Au, K. (2004). Multicultural factors and the effective instruction of students of diverse backgrounds. In A. Farstrup & S. Samuels (Eds.), *What research has to say about reading instruction* (pp. 392–413). Newark, DE. International Reading Association.

Au, K. H. (2007). Culturally responsive instruction: Application to multiethnic classrooms. *Pedagogies: An International Journal, 2*(1), 1–18.

Au, K. H. (2009/2010). Culturally responsive instruction: What is it, and how can we incorporate it in the classroom? *Reading Today, 27*(3), 30–31.

August, D., & Hakuta, K. (Eds.). (1997). *Improving schooling for language minority children: A research agenda.* Washington, DC: National Academy Press.

Banks, J. A. (1995). Multicultural education: Historical development, dimensions, and practice. In J. A. Banks & C. A. M. Banks (Eds.), *Handbook of research on multicultural education* (pp. 3–24). New York: Macmillan.

Banks, J. A. (1997). *Educating citizens in a multicultural society.* New York: Teachers College Press.

Banks, J. A. (2004). Multicultural education: Historical development, dimensions, and practice. In J. A. Banks & C. A. M. Banks (Eds.), *Handbook of research on multicultural education* (2nd ed., pp. 3–29). San Francisco: Jossey-Bass.

Beck, I. L., & McKeown, M. G. (2007). Increasing young low income children's oral vocabulary repertoires through rich and focused instruction. *Elementary School Journal, 107*, 251–271.

Belltech Systems. (2009). *DrawAnywhere.* Available at http://www. drawanywhere.com/about.aspx

Bender, W. N., & Shores, C. (2007). *Response to intervention: A practical guide for every teacher.* Thousand Oaks, CA: Corwin Press.

Berliner, D. (2009). *Poverty and potential: Out-of-school factors and school success.* Boulder, CO, and Tempe, AZ: Education and the Public Interest Center.

Bishop, R. S. (1992). Children's books in a multicultural world: A view from the USA. In E. Evans (Ed.), *Reading against racism* (pp. 19–38). Buckingham, England: Open University Press.

Bitz, M. (2004). The Comic Book Project: Forging alternative pathways to literacy. *Journal of Adolescent and Adult Literacy, 47*, 574–588.

Blachowicz, C., & Fisher, P. (2009). *Teaching vocabulary in all classrooms* (4th ed.). Upper Saddle River, NJ: Pearson/Merrill/Prentice Hall.

Blanchett, W., Klinger, J., & Harry, B. (2009). The intersection of race, culture, language, and disability: Implications for urban education. *Urban Education, 44*, 389–409.

boyd, d. (2007). Why youth (heart) social network sites: The role of networked publics in teenage social life. In D. Buckingham (Ed.), *Youth, identity, and digital media* (MacArthur Foundation Series on Digital Media and Learning, pp. 119–142). Cambridge, MA: MIT Press.

Bromley, K. (2007). Nine things every teacher should know about words and vocabulary instruction. *Journal of Adolescent and Adult Literacy, 50*, 528–537.

Callella, T. (2006). *I have, who has? Gr. 3–4 language arts.* Huntington Beach, CA: Creative Teaching Press.

Capps, R., Fix, M., Murray, J., Ost, J., Passel, J., & Herwantoro, S. (2005). *The new demography of America's schools: Immigration and the No Child Left Behind Act.* Washington, DC: The Urban Institute.

Carver, R. P. (1992). What do standardized tests of reading comprehension measure in terms of efficiency, accuracy, and rate? *Reading Research Quarterly, 27*, 346–359.

Chapman, I. T. (1994). Dissin' the dialectic on discourse surface differences. *Composition Chronicle, 7*(7), 4–7.

Chard, D. J., Vaughn, S., & Tyler, B. J. (2002). A synthesis of research on effective interventions for building reading fluency with elementary students with learning disabilities. *Journal of Learning Disabilities, 35*, 386–406.

Cho, K.-S., Ahn, K.-O., & Krashen, S. (2005). The effects of narrow reading of authentic texts on interest and reading ability in English as a foreign language. *Reading Improvement, 42*, 58–64.

Cummins, J., Bismilla, V., Chow, P., Cohen, S., Giampapa, F., Leoni, L., Sandhu, P., & Sastri, P. (2005). Affirming identity in multilingual classrooms. *Educational Leadership, 63*(1), 38–43.

Cunningham, P. M., & Allington, R. L. (1999). *Classrooms that work* (2nd ed.). New York: Longman.

Daneman, M. (1991). Individual differences in reading skills. In R. Barr, M. L. Kamil, P. Mosenthal, & P. D. Pearson (Eds.), *Handbook of reading research* (Vol. 2, pp. 512–538). White Plains, NY: Longman.

Darling-Hammond, L., & McLaughlin, M. W. (1995). Policies that support professional development in the era of reform. *Phi Delta Kappan, 76*, 597–604.

Delpit, L. (2002). No kinda sense. In L. Delpit & J. K. Dowdy (Eds.), *The skin that we speak* (pp. 31–48). New York: New York Press.

Dolch, E. (1955). *Methods in reading.* Champaign, IL: Garrard.

Dorr, R. (2006). Something old is new again: Revisiting language experience. *The Reading Teacher, 60*, 138–146.

DuFour, R., DuFour, R., Eaker, R., & Karhanek, G. (2004). *Whatever it takes: How professional learning communities respond when kids don't learn.* Bloomington, IN: National Education Service.

Duke, N. K., & Purcell-Gates, V. (2003). Genres at home and at school: Bringing the known to the new. *The Reading Teacher, 57*, 30–37.

Dunn, R. (1986). Learning style and its relation to exceptionality at both ends of the spectrum. *Exceptional Children, 4*, 496–506.

Echevarria, J., Vogt, M., & Short, D. (2010). *Making content comprehensible for elementary English learners: The SIOP model.* Boston: Allyn & Bacon.

Education for All Handicapped Children Act of 1975. (1975). 20 U.S.C. § 401.

Edwards, P. A. (2004). *Children's literacy development: Making it happen through school, family, and community involvement.* Boston: Allyn & Bacon.

Edwards, P. A., Pleasants, H., & Franklin, S. (1999). *A path to follow: Learning to listen to parents.* Portsmouth, NH: Heinemann.

Faltis, C. (2005). *Teaching English language learners in elementary school communities: A joinfostering approach* (5th ed.). Upper Saddle River, NJ: Prentice Hall.

Fisher, D., & Frey, N. (2008). *Better learning through structured teaching* Alexandria, VA: Association for Supervision and Curriculum Development.

Flocabulary: Hip-Hop in the Classroom. (2010). *The week in rap.* Available at http://theweekinrap.com

Foster, M. (1995). African American teachers and culturally relevant pedagogy. In J. A. Banks & C. A. M. Banks (Eds.), *Handbook of research on multicultural education* (pp. 570–581). New York, NY: Macmillan.

Fry, E. (1980). The new instant word list. *The Reading Teacher, 34*, 284–289.

Fry, E. (1998). The most common phonograms. *The Reading Teacher, 51*, 620–622.

Fuchs, D., & Fuchs, L. S. (2005). Responsiveness-to-intervention: A blueprint for practitioners, policy makers, and parents. *Teaching Exceptional Children, 28*(1), 57–61.

Garcia, G. E. (2003). The reading comprehension development and instruction of English language learners. In A. P. Sweet & C. E. Snow (Eds.), *Rethinking reading comprehension* (pp. 30–50). New York: Guilford Press.

Gardner, H. (1993). *Frames of mind: The theory of multiple intelligences.* London, England: Fontana.

Gardner, H. (1999). *Intelligence reframed: Multiple intelligences for the 21st century.* New York: Basic Books.

Gay, G. (2000). *Culturally responsive teaching: Theory, research, and practice.* New York: Teachers College Press.

Gee, J. P. (2004). *Situated language and learning: A critique of traditional schooling.* London, England: Routledge.

Genesee, F. (2005, January). *Literacy development in ELLs: What does the research say?* Paper presented at the annual meeting of the National Association for Bilingual Education. San Antonio, TX.

Gersten, R., & Baker, S. (2000). What we know about effective instructional practices for English language learners. *Exceptional Children, 66,* 454–470.

Goodinson, C. (2008–2010). *Pixton click and drag comics.* Available at http://pixton.com

Graves, A., Gersten, R., & Haager, D. (2004). Literacy instruction in multiple-language first-grade classrooms: Linking student outcomes to observed instructional practice. *Learning Disabilities Research & Practice, 19,* 262–272.

Greene, J. (1999). A meta-analysis of the Rossell and Baker review of bilingual education research. *Bilingual Research Journal, 21*(2, 3), 103–122.

Greene, S., & Abt-Perkins, D. (2003). *Making race visible: Literacy research for cultural understanding.* New York: Teachers College Press.

Guthrie, J. T., & Humenick, N. M. (2004). Motivating students to read: Evidence for classroom practices that increase reading motivation and achievement. In P. McCardle & V. Chhabra (Eds.), *The voice of evidence in reading research* (pp. 329–354). Baltimore, MD: Brookes.

Guthrie, J. T., Rueda, R. S., Gambrell, L. B., & Morrison, D. A. (2009). Roles of engagement, valuing, and identification in reading development of students from diverse backgrounds. In L. Morrow & R. S. Rueda (Eds.), *Handbook of reading and literacy among students from diverse backgrounds* (pp. 195–215). New York: Guilford Press.

Haggard, M. R. (1986). The vocabulary self-selection strategy: Using student interest and word knowledge to enhance vocabulary growth. *Journal of Reading, 29,* 634–642.

Hansen, A. L. (2005). *Hispanic student achievement.* Available at http://www.principalspartnership.com/success.pdf

Hansen, J. (1998). *When learners evaluate.* New York: Heinemann.

Heath, S. B. (1983). *Ways with words: Language, life, and work in communities and classrooms.* New York: Cambridge University Press.

Heath, S. B. (1994). The children of Trackton's children: Spoken and written language in social change. In R. B. Ruddell, M. R. Ruddell, &

H. Singer (Eds.), *Theoretical models and processes of reading* (4th ed., pp. 208–230). Newark, DE: International Reading Association.

Helman, L. A., & Burns, M. K. (2008). What does oral language have to do with it? Helping young English-language learners acquire a sight word vocabulary. *The Reading Teacher, 62,* 14–19.

Hidalgo, N. (1993). Multicultural teacher introspection. In T. Perry & J. Fraser (Eds.), *Freedom's plow: Teaching in the multicultural classroom* (pp. 99–106). New York: Routledge.

Hobbs, R. (1996). Expanding the concepts of literacy. In R. Kubey (Ed.), *Media literacy in the information age* (pp. 163–186). New York: Teachers College Press.

Hollins, E. R. (1996). *Culture in school learning: Revealing the deep meaning.* Mahwah, NJ: Erlbaum.

Hollins, E. R., King, J. E., & Hayman, W. C. (Eds.). (1994). *Teaching diverse populations: Formulating a knowledge base.* Albany, NY: State University of New York Press.

hooks, b. (1994). *Teaching to transgress: Education as the practice of freedom.* New York: Routledge.

Hopstock, P., & Stephenson, T. (2003). *Native languages of limited English proficient students.* Washington, DC: U.S. Department of Education.

Huffman, L. E. (1998). Spotlighting specifics by combining focus questions with K–W–L. *Journal of Adolescent and Adult Literacy, 41,* 470–479.

Ignite Learning, What causes Earth's seasons? (2006). Austin, TX: Ignite Learning. Available at http://www.ignitelearning.com

Igoa, C. (1995). *The inner world of the immigrant child.* Mahwah, NJ: Erlbaum.

Individuals with Disabilities Education Act Amendments of 2004, PL 108–446, 20 USC § 1400 et seq.

Jewitt, C. (2008). Multimodality and literacy in school classrooms. *Review of Research in Education, 32*(1), 241–267.

Kagan, S. (1994). *Kagan cooperative learning* (2nd ed.) San Clemente, CA: Kagan Publishing.

Kidder, T. (1990). *Among schoolchildren.* New York: Harper Perennial.

Kolb, D. A. (1976). *Learning Style Inventory.* Boston: Hay Group, Hay Resources Direct.

Kozol, J. (2001). *Ordinary resurrections: Children in the years of hope.* New York: Harper Perennial.

Krashen, S. (1996). *Under attack: The case against bilingual education.* Culver City, CA: Language Education Associates.

Krashen, S. (2004). *Let's tell the public the truth about bilingual education.* Available at http://www.sdkrashen.com/articles/tell_the_truth/index.html

Krashen, S., & Brown, C. L. (2007). *What is academic language proficiency?* Available at http://www.sdkrashen.com/articles/Krashen_Brown_ALP.pdf

Krashen, S., & McField, G. (2005). What works? Reviewing the latest evidence on bilingual education. *Language Learner, 1*(2), 7–10, 34.

Kress, G. (2003). *Literacy in the new media age.* London, England: Routledge.

Ladson-Billings, G. (1994). *The dreamkeepers: Successful teachers for African-American children.* San Francisco: Jossey-Bass.

Ladson-Billings, G. (1995a). But that's just good teaching! The case for culturally relevant pedagogy. *Theory into Practice, 34*(3), 159–165.

Ladson-Billings, G. (1995b). Multicultural teacher education: Research, practice, and policy. In J. A. Banks & C. A. M. Banks (Eds.), *Handbook of research on multicultural education* (pp. 747–759). New York: Macmillan.

Lankshear, C., & Knobel, M. (2003). *New literacies: Changing knowledge and classroom learning.* Buckingham, England: Open University Press.

Lankshear, C., & Knobel, M. (2006). *New literacies: Everyday practice and classroom learning* (2nd ed.). New York: Open University Press.

Lankshear, C., & Knobel, M. (2007). Sampling "the new" in new literacies. In C. Lankshear & M. Knobel (Eds.), *A new literacies sampler* (pp. 1–24). New York: Peter Lang.

Lenhart, A., Ling R., Campbell, S., & Purcell, K. (2010). *Teens and mobile phones* (Pew Internet & American Life Project). Available at http://www.pewinternet.org/Reports/2010/Teens-and-Mobile-Phones.aspx

Lervag, A., & Aukrust, V. G. (2010). Vocabulary knowledge is a critical determinant of the difference in reading comprehension growth between first and second language learners. *Journal of Child Psychology and Psychiatry, 5*, 612–620.

Leu, D. J., Jr., Kinzer, C. K., Coiro, J., & Cammack, D. W. (2004). Toward a theory of new literacies emerging from the Internet and other information and communication technologies. In R. B. Ruddell & N. Unrau (Eds.), *Theoretical models and processes of reading* (5th ed., pp. 1570–1613). Newark, DE: International Reading Association.

Mandeville, T. F. (1994). KWLA: Linking the affective and cognitive domains. *The Reading Teacher, 47*, 679–680.

Martin, M. O., Mullis, I. V. S., & Kennedy, A. M. (Eds.). (2007). *PIRLS 2006 technical report.* Chestnut Hill, MA: TIMSS & PIRLS International Study Center, Boston College.

Maslow, A. H. (1970). *Motivation and personality* (2nd ed.). New York: Harper & Row.

McGinley, W. J., & Denner, P. R. (1987). Story impressions: A pre-reading/writing activity. *Journal of Reading, 31*, 248–253.

Menchaca, V. D. (2000). Providing a culturally relevant curriculum for Hispanic children. *Multicultural Education, 8*(3), 18–20.

Meyer, L. (2000). Barriers to meaningful instruction for English learners. *Theory into Practice, 39*, 228–236.

Moll, L. C. (1994). Literacy research in community and classrooms: A sociocultural approach. In R. B. Ruddell, M. R. Ruddell, & H. Singer (Eds.), *Theoretical models and processes of reading* (4th ed., pp. 179–207). Newark, DE: International Reading Association.

Mortenson, G., & Relin, D. O. (2007). *Three cups of tea: One man's mission to promote peace . . . one school at a time.* New York: Penguin Books.

The National Clearinghouse for English Language Acquisition (NCELA) funded by the USDOE Department of English Language Acquisition. *The growing numbers of limited English proficient students 1995/96–2005/06.* Available at http://www.ncela.gwu.edu/files/uploads/4/GrowingLEP_0506.pdf

National Council of Teachers of English. (2006). *NCTE position paper on the role of English teachers in educating English language learners (ELLs).* Urbana, IL: Author. Available at http://www.ncte.org/positions/statements/teacherseducatingell

National Reading Panel. (2000). *Report of the National Reading Panel: Teaching children to read: Report of the subgroups.* Washington, DC: U.S. Department of Health and Human Services, National Institute of Health.

Newton, E., Padak, N. D., & Rasinski, T. V. (2008). *Evidence-based instruction in reading: A professional development guide to vocabulary.* Boston: Pearson.

Nieto, S. (1996). *Affirming diversity: The sociopolitical context of multicultural education* (2nd ed.). White Plains, NY: Longman.

Nieto, S. (1999). *The light in their eyes.* New York: Teachers College Press.

Nieto, S. (2010). *Language, culture, and teaching: Critical perspectives* (2nd ed.). New York: Routledge.

Ogle, D. M. (1986). K–W–L: A teaching model that develops active reading of expository text. *The Reading Teacher, 39,* 564–570.

Oller, D. K., & Eilers, R. (2002). *Language and literacy in bilingual children.* Clevedon, England: Multilingual Matters.

Orellana, M. F., & Hernandez, A. (1999). Talking the walk: Children reading environmental print. *The Reading Teacher, 52,* 612–619.

Pailliotet, A. W., Semali, L., Rodenberg, R. K., Giles, J. K., & Macaul, S. L. (2000). Intermediality: Bridging to critical media literacy. *The Reading Teacher, 54,* 208–219.

Passel, J. S., & Cohn, D. (2008). *U.S. population projections 2005–2050.* Washington, DC: Pew Research Center.

Payne, R. K., DeVol, P., & Smith, T. D. (2000). *Bridges out of poverty: Strategies for professionals and communities* (2nd ed.). Highlands, TX: Aha Process.

Planty, M., Kena, G., & Hannes, G. (Eds.). (2009) *The condition of education 2009 in brief* (NCES 2009-082). Washington, DC: U.S. Department of Education, Institute of Education Sciences, National Center for Education Statistics. Available at http://nces.ed.gov/pubs2009/2009082.pdf

Portes, P. R., & Salas, S. (2009). Poverty and its relation to development and literacy. In L. Morrow, R. Rueda, & D. Lapp (Eds.), *Handbook of research on literacy instruction: Issues of diversity, policy, and equity* (pp. 97–113). New York: Guilford Press.

Pressley, M. (2000). What should the instruction of comprehension be the instruction of? In M. L. Kamil, P. B. Mosenthal, P. D. Pearson, & R. Barr (Eds.), *Handbook of reading research* (Vol. 3, pp. 545–561). Mahwah, NJ: Erlbaum.

Pressley, M. (2002). Effective beginning reading instruction. *Journal of Literacy Research, 34,* 165–188.

Pressley, M., Allington, R., Wharton-McDonald, R., Block, C. C., & Morrow, L. M. (2001). *Learning to read: Lessons from exemplary first grades.* New York: Guilford Press.

The proud family. (2003). Culture shock [season 3, episode 3]. Burbank, CA: Walt Disney Studios.

Rasinski, T. V., & Padak, N. (2004). *3-minute reading assessments: Word recognition, fluency, and comprehension: Grades 1–4.* New York: Scholastic.

Rasinski, T. V., & Padak, N. (2005). *3-minute reading assessments: Word recognition, fluency, and comprehension: Grades 5–8.* New York: Scholastic.

Rasinski, T. V., & Padak, N. (2008a). *Evidence-based instruction in reading: A professional development guide to comprehension.* Boston: Pearson.

Rasinski, T. V., & Padak, N. D. (2008b). *From phonics to fluency: Effective teaching of decoding and reading fluency in the elementary school.* Boston: Pearson.

Rasinski, T. V., & Padak, N. (2008c). *3-minute reading assessments: Word recognition, fluency, and comprehension: Professional study guide.* New York: Scholastic.

Rasinski. T. V., Padak, N. D., & Fawcett, G. (2010). *Teaching children who find reading difficult* (4th ed.). Boston, MA: Pearson.

Renyi, J. (1998). Building learning into the teaching job. *Educational Leadership, 55*(5), 70–74.

Reyes, I., Wyman, L., Gonzales, N., Rubinstein-Avila, E., Spear-Ellinwood, K. C., Gilmore, P., & Moll, L. C. (2009). What do we know about discourse patterns of diverse students in multiple settings? In L. Morrow, R. Rueda, & D. Lapp (Eds.), *Handbook of research on literacy instruction: Issues of diversity, policy, and equity* (pp. 55–76). New York: Guilford Press.

Richard-Amato, P. A., & Snow, M. A. (2005). *Academic success for English Language Learners.* White Plains, NY: Longman.

Rico, J. (2010, March). *Keynote address.* Presented at the annual meeting of the Transition to Teaching Annual Project Directors and Evaluators meeting. Washington, DC.

Rideout, V., Foehr, U., & Roberts, D. (2010). *Generation M2: Media in the lives of 8- to 18- year olds: A Kaiser Family Foundation study.* Menlo Park, CA: Henry J. Kaiser Family Foundation.

Robins, K. N., Lindsey, R. B., Lindsey, D. B., & Terrell, R. (2005). *Culturally proficient instruction: A guide for people who teach* (2nd ed.). Thousand Oaks, CA: Corwin Press.

Rosen, L. (2010). *Rewired: Understanding the I generation and the way they learn.* New York: Palgrave Macmillan.

Samuels, S. (2002). Reading fluency: Its development and assessment. In A. Farstrup & S. Samuels (Eds.), *What research has to say about reading instruction* (pp. 166–183). Newark, DE: International Reading Association.

Schein, E. (1992). *Organizational culture and leadership.* San Francisco: Jossey-Bass.

Schmidt, P. R. (1998). The ABC's model: Teachers connect home and school. In T. Shanahan & F. V. Rodriguez-Brown (Eds.), *National Reading Conference yearbook* (Vol. 47, pp. 194–208). Chicago: National Reading Conference.

Schmidt, P. R. (1999). Know thyself and understand others. *Language Arts, 76,* 332–340.

Schmidt, P. R. (2002). *Cultural conflict and struggle: Literacy learning in a kindergarten program.* New York: Peter Lang.

Schmitt, N. (2008). Instructed second language vocabulary learning. *Language Teaching Research, 12,* 329–363.

Schon, D. (1984). *The reflective practitioner: How professionals think in action.* New York: Basic Books.

Short, D. J., & Fitzsimmons, S. (2007). *Double the work: Challenges and solutions to acquiring language and academic literacy for adolescent English language learners: A report to Carnegie Corporation of New York.* Washington, DC: Alliance for Excellent Education.

Sleeter, C. (2005). *Un-standardizing curriculum: Multicultural teaching in the standards-based classroom.* New York: Teachers College Press.

Sleeter, C. E., & Grant, C. (2009). *Making choices for multicultural education: Five approaches to race, class and gender* (6th ed.). Danvers, MA: John Wiley.

Smith, F. (1983). *Essays into literacy: Selected papers and some afterthoughts.* Exeter, NH: Heinemann.

Stahl, S. A., & Nagy, W. E. (2006). *Teaching word meanings.* Mahwah, NJ: Erlbaum.

Stauffer, R. G. (1980). *The language-experience approach to the teaching of reading* (2nd ed.). New York: Harper & Row.

Sussman, G. (2009). *Kids from chaos.* Available at http://www.edweek. org/ew/articles/2009/12/21/16sussman.h29.html?tkn=QPQCYgyXx QThoSGalWkBd2tajZEci9JiZTsb&cmp=clp-ascd

Tatum, A. W. (2000). Breaking down barriers that disenfranchise African American adolescents in low-level reading tracks. *Journal of Adolescent and Adult Literacy, 44,* 52–64.

Tatum, A. W., & Fisher, T. A. (2008). Nurturing resilience among adolescent readers. In S. Lenski & J. Lewis (Eds.), *Reading success for struggling adolescent learners* (pp. 58–73). New York: Guilford Press.

Taylor, B. M., Pearson, P. D., Clark, K., & Walpole, S. (2000). Effective schools and accomplished teachers: Lessons about primary-grade reading instruction in low-income schools. *Elementary School Journal, 101,* 121–165.

Teacher of the year: Education "must be learner centered." (2010, June). *eSchool News, 13*(6), 12.

Tierney, R. (1998). Literacy assessment reform: Shifting beliefs, principled possibilities, and emerging practices. *The Reading Teacher, 51*, 374–390.

U.S. Census Bureau. (2006). *The 2006 statistical abstract: Computers for school instruction in elementary and secondary schools.* Available at http://www.census.gov/compendia/statab/2010/tables/10s0254.xls

U.S. Census Bureau. (2008). *Age and sex in the United States: 2008: Population by age and sex.* Available at http://www.census.gov/population/www/socdemo/age/age_sex_2008.html

U.S. Department of Education. (2007). *Twenty-seventh annual report to Congress on the implementation of the Individuals with Disabilities Education Act, 2005.* Washington, DC: Author.

U.S. Department of Education, Institute of Education Sciences, National Center for Education Statistics. (n.d.). *Early Childhood Longitudinal Study.* Washington, DC: Author. Accessed at http://nces.ed.gov/ecls

U.S. Department of Education, Institute of Education Sciences, National Center for Education Statistics. (2001). *Fourth-grade reading highlights 2000.* Washington, DC: Author.

U.S. Department of Education, Institute of Education Sciences, National Center for Education Statistics. (2009a). *Digest of education statistics.* Washington, DC: Author. Available at http://nces.ed.gov

U.S. Department of Education, Institute of Education Sciences, National Center for Education Statistics. (2009b). *The nation's report card: Reading 2009: National Assessment of Educational Progress at grades 4 and 8* (NCES 2010–458). Washington, DC: Author.

Van Allen, R. (1982). *Language experience activities.* Orlando, FL: Houghton Mifflin.

VanDeWeghe, R. (2007). What about vocabulary instruction? *English Journal, 97*, 101–114.

Vaughn, S., & Fuchs, L. S. (2003). Redefining learning disabilities as inadequate response to instruction: The promise and potential problems. *Learning Disabilities Research & Practice, 18*(3), 137–146.

Walsh, M. (2008). Worlds have collided and modes have merged: Classroom evidence of changed literacy practices. *Literacy, 42*(2), 101–108.

Walther-Thomas, C. S. (1997). Co-teaching experiences: The benefits and problems that teachers and principals report over time. *Journal of Learning Disabilities, 30*, 395–407.

Warner, M., & Moore, R. (2008). What we learned from Arturo: Helping ELLs take part in classroom conversations. *English Leadership Quarterly, 30*(3), 14–15.

Wenglinsky, H. (2000). *How teaching matters: Bringing the classroom back into discussion of teacher quality.* Princeton, NJ: Educational Testing Service.

West, K. (1998). Noticing and responding to learners: Literacy evaluation and instruction in the primary grades. *The Reading Teacher, 51*, 550–559.

Whitaker, T. (2004). *What great teachers do differently: 14 things that matter most.* Larchmont, NY: Eye on Education.

Wiggins, G., & McTighe, J. (2005). *Understanding by design* (Expanded 2nd ed.). Upper Saddle River, NJ: Pearson Education.

Willig, A. (1985). A meta-analysis of selected studies on the effectiveness of bilingual education. *Review of Educational Research, 55,* 269–317.

Wisniewski, R., Padak, N. D., & Rasinski, T. V. (2011). *Evidence-based instruction in reading: A professional development guide to response to intervention.* Boston, MA: Pearson/Allyn & Bacon.

Xu, Y., & Drame, E. (2008). Culturally appropriate context: Unlocking the potential of Response to Intervention for English Language Learners. *Early Childhood Education, 35,* 205–311.

Zehr, M. A. (2010). Latino kindergartners' social skills found strong. *Education Week.* Available at http://www.edweek.org/ew/articles/2010/05/03/31latino-2.h29.html?tkn=LSSFnO6hl0DWLekFrdWMeEl5PCxZlkxG5hj8&cmp=clp-sb-ascd

Children's and Young Adults' Literature

Ackerman, K. (1992). *This old house.* New York: Atheneum.

Carle, E. (1997). *Today is Monday.* New York: Putnam.

Guarino, D. (1989). *Is your Mama a llama?* New York: Scholastic.

Janovitz, M. (1996). *Is it time?* New York: North South.

Kasza, K. (1987). *The wolf's chicken stew.* New York: Putnam.

Numeroff, L. (1985). *If you give a mouse a cookie.* New York: HarperCollins.

Patterson, J. (2007). *Maximum ride, Book 1: The angel experiment.* New York: Little, Brown.

Pizer, A. (1992). *It's a perfect day.* Upper Saddle River, NJ: Scott Foresman.

Speigelman, A., & Mouly, F. (Eds.). (2003). *Little lit: It was a dark and silly night.* New York: Joanna Colter.

Speigelman, A., & Mouly, F. (Eds.). (2006). *Big fat little lit.* New York: Puffin.

Speigelman, A., & Mouly, F. (Eds.). (2009). *The TOON treasury of classic children's comics.* New York: Abrams ComicArts.

Telgemeier, R., & Martin, A. M. (2006a). *The baby-sitter's club: Kristy's great idea.* New York: Graphix.

Telgemeier, R., & Martin, A. M. (2006b). *The baby-sitter's club: The truth about Stacey.* New York: Graphix.

Winter, J. (2008). *Barack.* New York: HarperCollins.